How Do We Tell
the Children?

How Do We Tell the Children?

A Parents' Guide to Helping Children Understand and Cope When Someone Dies

Dan Schaefer
and
Christine Lyons

NEWMARKET PRESS   NEW YORK

To our children:
Andrea, Daniel, Pamela, Mark, David, and Shawn Schaefer
and
Sean, Bridget, and Brendan Lyons

First Edition
1 2 3 4 5 6 7 8 9 0

Library of Congress Cataloging-in-Publication Data

Schaefer, Dan.
　How do we tell the children?

　Bibliography: p.
　Includes index.
　1. Children and death. 2. Death—Psychological aspects. 3. Bereavement—Psychological aspects. 4. Parent and child. I. Lyons, Christine. II. Title.
BF723.D3S33 1986　　155.9'37　　85-61816
ISBN 0-937858-60-9

Quantity Purchases
Companies, professional groups, clubs, and other organizations may qualify for special terms when ordering quantites of this title. For information, contact the Special Sales Department, Newmarket Press, 3 East 48th Street, New York, N.Y. 10017. Phone (212) 832-3575.

Designed by Levavi & Levavi

Manufactured in the United States of America

Acknowledgments

In the course of developing my program and this book, I received guidance and assistance from a great many people. I would like to thank the following: Alan J. Barnett, Ph.D., National Psychological Association for Psychoanalysis; John Brogan and Ula Maiden, Strang Middle School, Yorktown Heights, New York; Rudolph Calabrese, Ph.D.; Bruce Danto, M.D.; the Reverend Ingimar DeRidder, Brooklyn Baptist Church; the Reverend Edward Dougherty, Immaculate Conception Seminary, Huntington, New York; Hal Fishkin, M.D., Department of Child Psychiatry, Harlem Hospital Center, New York; Rabbi Jacob Goldberg, Rabbinical Bereavement Counseling Program of the New York Board of Rabbis; Janet Kamien, Boston Children's Museum; Elliot Kranzler, M.D., Department of Child Psychiatry, Columbia University College of Physicians and Surgeons, New York; Austin H. Kutscher, President, Foundation of Thanatology, Columbia University

257216

College of Physicians and Surgeons; Harriet Lainer; Leonard Levy; Richard Lonetto, Ph.D.; Otto S. Margolis, Ph.D., American Academy McAllister Institute of Funeral Services; Susan McCormick; the Reverend Luciano Padilla, Jr., Bay Ridge Christian Center, New York; David Peretz, M.D., Department of Psychiatry, Columbia University College of Physicians and Surgeons; Gwen Schwartz-Borden, C.S.W., Family Service Association, Nassau County, New York; the Reverend Mark Wilhelm, Bethany Lutheran Church, Brooklyn, New York.

In addition, I would especially like to thank the families I have assisted, whose confidence, trust, sharing, and encouragement have made this book possible.   —D. S.

Thanks to William Cole, Anne Crosman, Irving Danker, Jack Kennington, C.S.S.R., and Simon Perchik for their kindness and help.   —C. L.

Special thanks to our publisher, Esther Margolis, our agent, Felicia Eth, and our editor, Katherine Heintzelman, who helped craft a complicated topic.

Contents

Foreword

by David Peretz, M.D.

Three years ago, I heard Dan Schaefer speak to an audience of health professionals and educators concerned with dying, death, and bereavement. His point of view had developed as an outgrowth of meeting with bereaved families in their acute grief in the funeral setting. His presentation was remarkable for its sensitivity, openness, and simplicity. Here was a funeral director who was totally committed to helping families in a time of terrible stress, and who had the gift of caring about the most vulnerable members of the family—the children.

Dan's work with families in acute grief convinced him that children were often either gently shunted aside, avoided, or misinformed with "cover stories" by bereaved parents, relatives, and friends. Many bereaved adults find the effort of listening to their children and communicating with them openly about their loss and grief almost more than they can bear. This is intensified by fears of hurting or upsetting the child, saying or doing something wrong. They are not aware that it could be more harmful to avoid the subject, to "protect" the child from the facts of death, than to deal with them in a simple, straightforward manner. Dan Schaefer gradually realized the pernicious short- and long-term effects that such avoidance, neglect, and misinformation could have upon children. And like the pioneer he is, he set out to do something about the problem. The funeral chapel was his setting, and his generous heart and inquiring mind his research instruments. His added strength lay in his straightforwardness. He was unencumbered by professional jargon or theories about human behavior. He began, as most outstanding clinicians begin, with simple observation.

Meeting with hundreds, and ultimately thousands, of parents and their children provided him with a broad range of experience. He talked to toddlers and preschoolers, young children and adolescents, and found each of them likely to have specific concerns based on their relationship to the person who had died and on their dependency needs, according to age and circumstance. He learned that there are patterns of thought and imagination common to children at particular stages in their development, and that these patterns are reflected in the kinds of questions children ask.

On the basis of these conversations, observations, and experiences, Dan worked out a commonsense approach to talking with children about death. He checked it out with educators, psychologists, psychiatrists, clergy, and other professionals who had formed a new discipline—that of thanatology, the study of dying, death, and bereavement. Dan found a good fit between what these professionals knew about children's needs and what he had discovered as approaches to those needs. I had been working in thanatology since 1966, and when I heard Dan's presentation of his approach in

1982, I said to myself, "Here's an original." I went up to Dan at the conclusion of the presentations, congratulated him, and said, "You've got to write a book!" He looked at me, a little startled, and replied, "I've been thinking about it." When he called me two years later to tell me that he was, in fact, working on the book, I was delighted. I am even more delighted with the end result of that labor.

It is my belief that children thrive in a climate of realism: realistic limits, realistic demands made upon them in tune with their growing capacities, and realistic answers to their questions, pitched to the level of their understanding. This can best be provided in an atmosphere where parents listen respectfully to their children. Genuine listening requires being prepared to make new discoveries and to share sorrow and fear. This is difficult at any time; it is most difficult when the parent is in grief.

The very young approach life as naturalists, open-minded and curious. Unfortunately, their early experiences with death and the reactions of those around them frequently close down their openness and curiosity, leading to avoidance and denial. A child's first questions about death are an attempt to gain mastery over frightening images of abandonment, separation, loneliness, pain, and bodily damage. If we err on the side of overprotecting them from emotional pain and grief with "kind" lies, we risk weakening their coping capacities. Children will absorb our defensiveness, avoidance, denial, and general unwillingness to discuss death directly. Death becomes, quite literally, something unspeakable.

How Do We Tell the Children? makes it clear that when children are confronted with death or ask questions about it, they can and should be informed, simply and honestly and without overelaboration. With an eloquent simplicity, it demonstrates how parents can deal with their children's concepts, as well as their questions. If we are to encourage the growth of realistic thinking in our children, if we are to help them overcome the fear of death as violent and mutilating, we must engage in a dialogue with them. A parent's voice and image, valued and respected by the child, discussing death in a simple and honest way, is internalised for a lifetime as a source of strength and comfort in facing loss and grief. This book will, I believe, help parents find their voice to speak to their children. In so doing, they will be giving their children an invaluable gift.

DAVID PERETZ, M. D.
Department of Psychiatry, Columbia University
College of Physicians and Surgeons
Faculty, Columbia University Psychoanalytic
Center for Training and Research
Editor in Chief, *Advances in Thanatology*

Introduction:
The Solitary Mourner

On any day around four o'clock you could set your watch by them—Michael and his grandfather, walking down the street, hand in hand, to the corner store. Michael and Grandpa, the young and the old—best friends. They shared a two-family house in an outlying section of New York City; the old man lived upstairs, Michael and his parents downstairs. It had been that way since the child was born. When Michael was about seven, his family moved to Long Island, leaving Grandpa back in the city. "See you on Thanksgiving!" they all said. Thanksgiving came and went; no Grandpa. Same with Christmas. "Grandpa's away for awhile." Michael's parents explained. "Don't worry about it." Months went by and the child waited. Finally, when his birthday came and Grandpa didn't even send a card, Michael knew something was up. What could he have done to make Grandpa not love him anymore?

1

It was two years before Michael's parents told him what had really happened—that his grandfather had died shortly after they moved to Long Island. "I know they thought they were doing the right thing," Michael says now. "But it was a terrible time for me. They certainly didn't spare me any pain while I was wondering what had happened. And then when they finally told me the truth, I still had to deal with the feeling of losing Grandpa."

Whenever someone close to the family dies, each and every member of that family is affected. For the first few days, many parents have told me, they felt numb and drained by their grief, as though someone had pulled the plug and sucked all the energy out of them. It's an overwhelming, stressful time, and there are so many details to attend to— funeral arrangements to be made, relatives to be notified. And all of this when you feel like a videotape running in slow motion, out of synch. For many people, the support they receive during this difficult period is crucial, helping them hold their world together. Neighbors stop by and bring in food. Relatives gather and minister to each other, sometimes after years of being separated. People cry and reminisce and comfort each other in their loss, and grief is allowed to flow.

Very often, though, the children in the family are shut out of this support network, given inaccurate or incomplete information and not included in the activities that can be such a necessary part of coping with a death. The fortunate ones, whom the network does support and nurture, are what I call "inside kids"; those, like Michael, whom the network ignores are "outside kids." "Outside kids" feel abandoned, lonely, angry, and confused.

This came home to me for the first time about nine years ago. I was sitting in the office of my family funeral home in Brooklyn when a nine-year-old boy walked in. "My uncle out there," he said, pointing to the viewing room,

"Why did he die?" I was really taken aback. "I think you'd better talk to your parents about that," I said. But as I sat there watching him walk out, I was filled with sympathy for the child. No one had told him what had happened. I realized that his parents probably didn't know what to say, and I thought— how alone that boy must feel!

I've worked with more than 3,000 parents during the days just after a death, and one thing I know for sure—many people find it almost impossible to talk with their children about death. "How do we tell the children?" they ask. "I can talk to them about sex or drinking or drugs . . . just about anything. But when it comes to talking about death, forget it."

There are a number of reasons for this. First, there's the philosophy "Let kids be kids." Parents tell me that they don't want to worry their children with problems, that they'll have enough to worry about when they get older; that their children are too young to understand and that, before you know it, they'll forget that the person even existed.

Many parents opt not to deal with the situation because they don't want to put their children *or* themselves through unnecessary pain. As Jeannie said several days after her father's funeral, "I simply couldn't bear to watch my little Evan crying and talking about how much he missed his grandpa. And I didn't want my mother to have to go through that either. It's my own feelings I'm trying to protect. I know that. But I just can't handle it right now."

Children say what they think and feel, honestly and openly, and in their directness our protection is stripped away. They say things that force us to confront the loss straight on, to deal with the emotional reality of a situation. When someone dies we're suddenly confronted with our own mortality, something that we never talk about, something that most of us are afraid to think about.

Andrew comes from a very close family that believes in sheltering children from the unpleasant things in life. When he was about six, his cousin, whom he often played with, all of a sudden disappeared. "Don't worry," said one of the relatives, "he'll come back some day." Andrew remembers waiting and waiting for his cousin, wondering when he'd be coming back. Several years later, he realized that his little friend had died. "They weren't really trying to lie to me," Andrew says now, looking back on that time. "Their story was partially true, because our family believes that at the end of the world everyone does come back. They were just using a gimmick to try to help me."

Helping young people cope better is what we're all interested in. But avoiding the issue or making up fairy tales to explain away death are devices that almost always fall apart. Saying Grandpa's away on a camping trip while all the relatives are moving in and out of the house in various stages of grief is a charade that the youngster will soon get wise to. Even a three-year-old will sense that something is happening.

Children know when we're bothered or afraid to talk about something. They pick up the unspoken vibrations that all is not well. The mood of the house has a certain cadence to it, a certain rhythm. Every day your child gets a consistent message that things go along and that people act in a certain way. Then one day all that changes.

Jimmy's mother sat in my office making arrangements for her husband's funeral.

"What have you said to your children?" I asked her.

"The two oldest know their father died. I don't think I'll tell the little guy."

"Is he at home right now?"

"Yes."

"Are the bigger kids all upset?"

"Of course."

"What do you think little Jimmy thinks is going on?"

"He keeps asking about his daddy."

"What do you say?"

"I tell him he's still very sick."

"Is everyone acting the same way they did when he was sick?"

"No, the older ones are really upset. . . . Do you think the little guy knows?"

Certainly, an adult is better equipped than a child to cope with a death in the family. Armed with years of experience that help cushion the blow, adults are also privy to the facts—what really happened, what's going to happen. That knowledge and experience give us comfort in our loss. We've been through times of pain and we know they don't last forever.

Children, on the other hand, have no idea what to expect as far as death and grief are concerned. If they have not been given an explanation of what happened—or if they can't believe or understand the explanation they have been given— they will use what little information they can get to construct their own story about why the people around them are so upset. Very often what a youngster creates is a wild fantasy, much worse than the facts. Thought not mature enough to handle the bad news, he becomes anxious and fearful. "Something bad happened. What did I do? Maybe everyone's upset because I wet my bed last week!" If he's been given an inadequate explanation and senses a cover-up, he'll figure that he's dealing with something dangerous and unknown.

That's what happened with Jerry when he was a youngster. Now in his mid-twenties, he says he remembers his grandmother's death as clearly as if it were yesterday.

"My grandmother was ill at home, and the family was all around her when she died. I was immediately taken across the street to a neighbor's house, never allowed to see Grandmother, to be with the others, or to go to the funeral. I remember running and hiding under the bed after they left. I couldn't understand why I had to be alone while everyone else was together somewhere else. I kept thinking that since they wouldn't let me come to see her, how horrible she must look! Nobody told me what was going on. It took a long time before I could forgive my parents."

Another man I talked with, a middle-aged rabbi whose father died when he was seven, still remembers the family gathered in the living room, wailing. "I didn't know what it meant. I was so alone and afraid. And for years I used to have daydreams that my father would come back."

Psychiatrist Bruce Danto of Fullerton, California, says that keeping a child in the dark when there's a death is often a kind of humiliation for the youngster. "The way it comes across to the child is, 'Look, kid, you bother me. You're in the way. You're not entitled to know what's going on here.' "

When this happens, the child is put into the unhappy position of being a "solitary mourner." One of the saddest things to see is a casket in a church or funeral home with just one mourner beside it. I've actually seen people drop into church for a quick visit, then change their plans and stay for the funeral when they see someone they don't even know sitting up front alone by a casket. No one wants to let a person grieve alone. And yet this is exactly what happens to many children when someone they have been close to dies.

A final reason that we find it so difficult to talk to our children about death is that we just don't know what to say. We're not very comfortable with the idea of death ourselves, and we often use euphemisms to hide our discomfort. We're especially unprepared to discuss it in terms that children can understand, and to answer the myriad questions that children always have.

A child's mind does not work the same way as an adult's. Less sophisticated, it processes information about subjects like death differently. This sounds obvious, but it's surprisingly easy to forget. One parent said to me recently, "I told Valerie, 'Your cousin died,' that's all. She knows what that means." But does she? Does she know what "dead" means? Does she know why the person died, and what's going to happen to the body? These sorts of questions are on the minds of most children who are faced with a death, and they need answers.

Although death is still treated by many as a taboo subject, when Will Lee, the actor who played Mr. Hooper on TV's "Sesame Street," died several years ago, the show's producers took the opportunity to explain the death to their young viewers. "We felt we ought to deal with it head-on. If we left it unsaid, the kids would notice," producer Dulcy Singer explained in an interview at the time. "Our instincts told us to be honest and straightforward." After consulting with a child psychologist, the "Sesame Street" writers prepared a script designed to answer some basic questions a pre-schooler would have. "Who's going to take care of the store?" asks Big Bird, the show's representative five-year-old. "Who's going to make me birdseed milkshakes and tell me stories?" David, the neighborhood's father, answers, "We'll all tell you stories and make sure you're okay." "It won't be the same," says the grieving Big Bird.

Susan seemed to be a textbook example of how to handle children when someone close to them dies. When her husband was killed, she kept her cool and pulled her children in close to her. A very down-to-earth, sensible woman, she gave the straight story to any questions the children asked, explaining what had happened to their father, including them in the wake and funeral, and telling them if they had any further questions, they should ask—she'd explain what she could. But after a few months went by, Susan realized that she was missing some important information. "It wasn't enough to just explain how their father died," she told me. "I had to learn to help them cope with their feelings of loss, and I had no way of knowing what was going on in their heads."

Susan was prepared with the right attitude for marvelous parent-child communication. By instinct, she knew part of the message she needed to send—openness, honesty, the freedom to ask questions and to grieve. But she was lacking a lot of the information we'll give you in this book—a how-to rundown on talking with children of all ages about death; what they think and understand, how they feel, and how you can help them cope with their feelings.

The program that I will outline grew out of my experience talking with thousands of families who have come to my funeral home, as well as consultations with psychologists, social workers, and other counseling professionals, and lectures I've given at workshops and symposia dealing with children and grief. The book is divided into chapters that will tell you what children aged two and up already know and are capable of understanding about death; what words to use when explaining death, including special situations such as accident and illness; and how to help your child deal with grief. In addition, there is a special Crisis Section at the back of the book that distills much of this information into a ready reference for answering specific questions that come up. This program has worked for a lot of different people in a lot of different circumstances. You may not relate to everything in this book, but I think you'll find that much of it will help.

Unlike other parenting guides, where if you look at the picture long enough you'll eventually learn how to change a diaper, you'll have to take the information I give you and tailor it to your own situation. But you won't be going it alone—you'll be part of a large group of parents who have broken the communication barrier and helped their children feel more at ease talking about the feelings that surround death.

1.

What Children Think
About Death

To communicate with children effectively, we have to know what they are thinking—what's going in their minds. It's our responsibility as communicators to package our message so that our listeners will understand what we're trying to tell them. And we have to appreciate the child's level of development and what he or she already knows about death before we can structure what we're going to say. The message to a four-year-old will obviously be very different from one we'd give to a teenager, but in both cases it must be finely tuned, gently presented, and double-checked so that we're sure it has been received in the way we intended— that the child got the story straight. If we package the message well, then we can control it. That makes it a lot easier on both us and our children during a time of crisis. The children will be dealing with adults who feel confident about what they are saying; and we parents will be straightforward, in charge, giving our children the information they need.

(1) One thing children *don't* need is to be loaded down with all the scientific information and explicit details about how the person died . . . at least not at the beginning. A simple explanation is what you're aiming for.

(2) Assessing the situation, looking at the age and maturity of the child, will help determine how much he or she can handle. In this chapter we'll show you how to do that by giving some guidelines on the ways children think at different ages. You decide what best fits your child, and then you'll be able to construct the right message for him or her.

(3) Start by asking yourself some questions. What kind of experience has he or she had with death? If you've had a pet that died, you have a starting point, something to relate to a person's death. Of course, you must be sure the child understands that the death of an animal is very different from that of a human being. Perhaps the pet had to be "put to sleep" (a euphemism that should *not* be used, as we'll discuss later; the child should be told instead that the pet had to be killed in order to end its suffering). If so, you must make it clear that we don't do that with people. But if the death of a pet is handled well—if the child is told exactly what is happening to the animal and why, and if he or she is given the opportunity to remember the pet with a backyard "burial service," or perhaps just with long discussions of the good times they had together and how bad it feels—then it can give you a starting point for any future encounters with death, among friends or in the family.

(4) In addition, a child's thinking is very much influenced by his surroundings, colored by what he sees and what he hears. Just consider what the average youngster sees on TV. The coyote chasing Roadrunner gets mashed, maimed, and flattened, only to pop up and start racing around again. Hun-

dreds of people die each year on the news programs. The cops-and-robbers shows do away with several bad guys per night. Children even act out death as they're playing: "Bang, bang, you're dead!" Some parents, when the suggestion is made that they talk to their children about death, protest that they don't want to expose them to such a difficult thing. And yet children are absorbing death all the time! Just as we can't follow them around protecting them for the rest of their lives, so we can't shelter them from the idea of death.

Given the fact that the youngster knows there is such a thing as death, what does he or she understand about this particular death facing you now? Did he or she know the person was sick? Was there a lingering illness, or a sudden heart attack? For an adult who watched Grandpa slowly deteriorate, the experience had a continuity—sick, sicker, sickest—and the death was not unexpected. But for a child who didn't know how sick Grandpa was, that death had the shocking effect of a sudden tragedy. If the child has been given straightforward reports—Grandpa's getting worse, he's not getting better, he may die—he or she will be a bit more prepared when the crisis comes.

Did the child know Grandpa was old? For a youngster, whose frame of reference is different from that of an adult, Mommy and Daddy are very old.

Was Grandpa killed in an accident? What happened? What kind of information does the child have about how the death occurred? Those parents who just say "He died" leave a lot to the child's imagination. What might other people have told him about what happened? And what might he have over-heard? One woman I know, who was nine when her mother died, remembers lying in her bedroom listening to the grown-ups whispering in the living room. One of her friends had told her that a poisonous smell had killed her mother. And so she lay there imagining that she too was dying, and the relatives were whispering, afraid to tell her.

"Whispers are terrible to a child," says child psychiatrist Hal Fishkin, who works with bereaved children in New York City. "Whispers, secrets, fairy tales. . . . It's really condescending, patronizing, to assume children can't deal with the traumas we can. Having experienced some major losses without data in my own life, I can tell you it's a rather mind-maiming experience. It makes you come up with conclusions in your own little head that are not consonant with reality, and you always come up on the short end of the stick. Something terrible's happened and it's all your fault. The fantasy is always worse than the reality."

One way to find out just what your youngsters are thinking is by listening to them explain what has happened to another child. "Grandma's walking the earth," one seven-year-old told another, obviously very upset about possibly having the ghost drop in for a visit. Where did she ever get such an idea? The mother finally found out that in religion class the child had heard something about spirits walking the earth. The little girl put that together with the opening on a TV show that shows a man sitting up in a casket, and she had the makings of a wild and scary misconception about death. Fortunately, her mother overheard that conversation, and she gave the child the facts and eased her mind. "That only happens in the movies. It's make-believe—just like Superman flying."

Sometimes as I explain my program to people they point out that I'm talking like a child. Well, that's just the point. You don't speak in German if you're talking to a Frenchman. You have to stoop down or put the child on your lap, look into his eyes, and talk to him in his language. Listen to your child carefully and sympathetically, as you would to a good friend going through a crisis, looking beyond the words.

Listen with the heart. Dr. Hal Fishkin says that "forcing yourself to walk in his moccasins will yield the right way to go when you're trying to talk with a child. Find out what he knows and what he's experienced, and you can pretty well guess what some of his ideas and feelings are."

In my own experience working with children and their parents, I've found that although each child is, of course, a unique individual, there are certain things you can predict that most children will say. A child of a certain age thinks in a certain way; this is not true of all of them, of course, but it's true enough for us to make some generalizations. One of these generalizations is that children think about and are concerned about death.

In *How It Feels to Be a Child*, Carole Klein points out that studies show a high percentage of children (eighty percent) think about death. They wrestle with fears about it without telling their parents, burying their thoughts and feelings inside, just as their parents do. That's surprising to many adults, who assume that if a child doesn't talk about something he or she is not thinking about it. Not long ago I had the following conversation with seven-year-old Leon.

"My grandma died last year," Leon said to me.

"Oh, it must have been very hard for you. Were you close?"

"Yes, she lived with us since I was a baby and took care of me when Mommy went to work."

"You must have had a lot of fun with Grandma."

"Sure. She used to read to me a lot. We had a lot of fun."

"Did you tell anyone you missed her?" I asked.

"Well, every time I talked about Grandma everyone would cry. So I stopped. . . ."

"Do you think a lot about dying?"

"Yes, but not me dying."

"Well, who?"

"My parents. I'm afraid a lot. I don't like Mommy and Daddy to go out without me."

"Have you ever told anyone?"

"Only you. Nobody wants to talk to me about it."

Remember that a child usually builds his whole world around his mother and father. They are the ones who take care of him, feed him, hug him. A very young child can grasp only what he sees, his known world. If you talk to him about dying, of someone going away and not coming back, his mind frequently turns to his parents, and he becomes afraid that they too are going to die.

Very often when a child hears something he misunderstands what is being said. Then, to complicate matters, when he can't understand something or doesn't have enough information to bring his ideas to a logical conclusion, he often makes up the part of the message that's missing. With lack of information, his reasoning becomes twisted.

Psychiatrist Bruce Danto points out that children sometimes get some pretty strange ideas just by watching things happen around them. "The thing that children will notice is that somebody doesn't look well . . . that 'Grandpa's not playing with me. Why is Grandpa so pale?' " Now if Grandpa is at home, getting intravenous feeding, and it's not explained to the children that those tubes are there to help put medicine into Grandpa, the young child can be very frightened. "That's not my Grandpa who used to be around here. That's Grandpa the monster!"

As I said, there are certain ways of thinking and acting that are unique to children at various stages of development. While many of the characteristics overlap, four distinct groups and levels of development can be seen: two- to six-year-olds; six- to nine-year-olds; nine- to twelve-year-olds; and teenagers.

TWO TO SIX YEARS

Stop for a moment and watch a preschooler at play. To him or her the world is a magical place, full of people coming and going around the family, the center of the world. It's a world in transition, a time of learning and growing and finding out how things work. Concepts like time and death are not yet fully developed in the preschooler's mind; he simply can't grasp them. What he can understand are the day-to-day things in life, and the feeling of his family taking care of him.

Since a young child's experience and vocabulary are limited, he has to draw on what he knows. Imitating the world around him, he picks up Mommy's pocketbook or puts on Daddy's shoes, trying to see how a grownup feels, experimenting with words he hears to see how it all fits. "I'm going to work now!", the little child asserts as he shuffles down the hall.

Young children are equally sensitive to our nonverbal attitudes. If we are reserved, fearful, paranoid, or hostile, very often our children will pick up on those feelings and act just like us. If we are open, honest, warm, and loving, they will get the message that that's the way to be.

Children in this age group generally do not think of death as final; to them, *death is reversible*. In order to understand the finality of death, a youngster has to recognize that he is a separate person from his parents—that without them he can still exist. While older children can comprehend this, most preschoolers cannot. They are helpless by themselves, dependent, and they know they need to be protected. A world without his parents is beyond his grasp. His mind also can't imagine the nothingness of death. So, if he hears that someone dies, he figures it's a temporary thing; you die and then come back; it's like going out to the grocery store. Just as characters on TV disappear on one show and appear on another, so will Grandpa rise from the dead. He's really dead only for a little time. He's still eating and moving around; it's just that he now happens to be underground or up in the sky somewhere. Whatever Grandpa happened to be doing when we last saw him, he's still doing it now.

One little fellow, Roy, age five, was on his first airplane trip when he asked his mother to open the window. "I want to give JoJo some dinner," he explained. Roy's thinking was that the plane was flying around heaven and that his friend JoJo, who had died a few months before, was hiding behind one of the clouds, alive and well and hungry. His sister Fredericka, just a year older, described how JoJo got up to heaven: "The angels came down and got JoJo, and like E.T. she rose up into heaven one night. There had to be a whole bunch of angels to hold her because JoJo was so big."

Magical thinking plays a big role in children's lives at this age, and of course it extends to their thoughts about death. Some young children, for example, imagine that by putting a body in water, you'll bring it back to life, like a dehydrated food. Others figure that if they wish hard enough they can bring the dead person back to life.

Sometimes they even invest themselves with magical powers. "I'll go beat up the bad man who killed Auntie!" The child in his imagination fashions a set of powers that counters all the disquieting facts he's seen around him.

It's partly because of the magical world they create that youngsters get the courage to deal with the problems of life; but sometimes they go a little overboard. Consider the little girl who was playing in her grandmother's yard, bouncing the ball against the wall, over and over. In exasperation the grandmother yelled, "Stop doing that! You'll be the death of me yet!" The child thought about that for a moment, then started playing something else. A few days later Grandma died. "Boy, I've done it now!" The child thought she had killed her grandmother.

Connecting events that don't belong together is something children commonly do that many adults find hard to understand. In the example I just gave, the little girl connected the bouncing ball incident and the death of her grandmother, which filled her with guilt and a feeling of responsibility. Since most youngsters have a hard time admitting that they threw the ball that broke a window, you can imagine how hard it would be to tell someone that she killed her grandmother! That's why it's important to get to her and explain what really happened to Grandma before she distorts the incident out of all proportion in her mind. Adults seldom make these kinds of connections because their reasoning powers are developed. But children who are searching for a beginning, middle, and end to a story will fill in the blanks and simply make up a message when they're missing the facts.

They also take the admonitions of adults quite literally. "You have to eat so your body will get big and strong." That's what four-year-old Tim was told as he made soup out of his mashed potatoes one evening. The next morning his father died. Strange as it may seem, the child thought he had killed his father by not eating his potatoes. In another instance, Jimmy overheard Aunt Millie, saying that Grandpa had died in his sleep. "Thank God, it was so peaceful. He just fell asleep and died." When it came time for Jimmy to go to bed that night he wanted no part of it; he was afraid that he wouldn't wake up either.

A child hears that Grandpa got sick and died, and the next time Daddy starts to cough or the child himself gets a stomach pain, watch his reaction. "What color shirt was Grandpa wearing when he died?", he might ask. Tell him a blue one (without explaining that it had nothing to do with Grandpa's death), then see what happens the next time you try to put his blue pullover on him.

One middle-aged friend of mine, who has more gray hairs than he would like, could not understand why his grandson clung to him so tightly. He asked the child what was the matter. The reply: "You're very old, too [the gray hair], and I don't want you to die!"

Another little boy, named Brett, overheard that his grandfather had looked awful for the past few weeks, and he filed that away. A week later the child was watching a Saturday afternoon monster movie, in which some humanoid was melting across the screen. His mother came in and said, "Oh, I can't let you watch that. That's awful-looking!", and she switched off the TV. "Aha!" said the child to himself, and his mind connected three events. Here's how the syllogism went in his mind: 1) Grandpa looked awful; he died, and Mommy wouldn't let me go to see him; 2) That humanoid looked awful, and Mommy wouldn't let me watch him on TV; 3) Grandpa must look as horrible as that monster on TV. And that's the final picture the youngster retained of the grandfather he loved so much.

For parents to help their children, they must be aware that things like this may be going on in their heads. The experience of death is probably new and strange to them, and their feelings of confusion and guilt when someone they were close to dies may be absolutely overwhelming.

SIX TO NINE YEARS

Children who are around the ages of six to nine often look on death as a *taker*, something violent that comes and gets you, like a burglar or a ghost. When they hear that someone died, these children may ask, "Who killed him?" In their minds death is personified, an external agent that catches you. It's a scary skeleton or a bogeyman to be run away from or to be handled by magic.

Although children in this age group have begun to comprehend the finality of death, very often they retain a lot of that magical thinking, overestimating the power of their thoughts and wishes. They may accept the fact that someone has died and that it's final, but they don't accept the fact that it must happen to everyone, especially themselves.

Many children of this age are afraid that death is *contagious*, something that can be caught, like a cold. Some even think that if another child's parent dies they can catch death by playing with that child, or by playing in the house where the dead person lived. Little phrases and chants that they hear can have a traumatic effect on them. The bedtime verse that used to be so popular—"Now I lay me down to sleep, I pray the Lord my soul to keep; if I should die before I wake, I pray the Lord my soul to take"—caused many youngsters to worry about dying in their sleep. In order to get that fantasy material that is so scary to them out where we can help them deal with it, we have to get them to talk about it.

Still in a transitional stage, children aged six to nine find many words confusing. Some words have several meanings, and often the child can't differentiate between them. Take the word "soul," for example. One researcher told the story of a child caught in a fantasy who thought he heard his dead father speaking to him from a shoe box in the closet. In the child's mind, "soul" and the "sole" of a shoe had become all mixed up.

NINE TO TWELVE YEARS

As a child grows in the nine-to-twelve age group, he or she develops an acute sense of morality, of right and wrong behavior. Very often children will think of death as a *punishment* for bad behavior; an unkind person's death was due to his wrongdoing. Though they're making the transition to a more adult understanding of the concept of death, they will sometimes have remnants of magical thinking and the "I did it" syndrome. The child who resisted going to see his grandmother when she was sick, thinking, "Why do I have to go to see her? I'm missing my ball game. If only she wasn't around!", may be plagued with guilt when she dies. He probably wouldn't admit it to anyone, and it would take some detective work to find out that that's what he's thinking—but it's important to children know that wishes don't kill. You might start out by saying, "Some children think that a person can die if you just think about their dying," and see how your child responds.

At this age children will probably be interested in the biological details of what happened. Unlike younger children, they have a frame of reference now and can handle much of the information you would give an adult. Because of their schooling in science, some preteens understand more about the biology and chemistry of the body than we adults do.

Because they are experimenting with ideas and theories, they may think that death is a way of getting rid of people, to make ready for new ones. Another theory you hear among children in these "middle years" is that each time there's a death, there's a birth.

Their cognitive and emotional skills are in transition, and children this age have standards and concerns that are very important to them, such as the idea that when something dies it should be buried. Preteens often handle the funeral of a pet with great ceremony and ritual. Elaine, a twelve-year-old whose guinea pig died, seemed to express the same degree of concern for the burial of her pet as another child did for her father who had died six months earlier. Elaine was quite concerned about all the details—that it be buried in the "right place" in the yard, that the shoe box it was being buried in was clean, and so on.

Children in this age group have usually gone beyond wondering what death is. They're more caught up in questions of relationship. "Grandpa won't be able to go fishing with me anymore." "Who's going to take care of Grandma now?" "What's going to happen to our family now that he has died?" Concerned with practical things, the child wonders if the family's style of life will change; who will run the house, or make the money.

> "Why did you put all those good clothes on my father? It's a terrible waste of money."
> "Why is that?"
> "Well, all the dirt's going to get on him when he's buried."
> "You know, we close the casket before it's buried."
> "Oh, I didn't know that."

You might have thought that a pre-adolescent would know that when a casket is put in the ground the top is closed. But you can't assume that a child knows the same things as an adult. Also, in a stressful situation surrounding a death, children who might otherwise be very mature in their thinking may regress to an earlier stage of emotional response.

None of these stages that we are talking about is set in stone. Children move back and forth among them. Child psychiatrist Hal Fishkin thinks this process continues all the way through adulthood—that we are never entirely out of one stage and into another. "I think if you scratch most of the people you know, myself included, you'll find a residue of magical thinking. And when it comes to death, you'll have children who, because of the better education today, seem to be very mature, who know more about death, but who respond emotionally in a very infantile way. It's up to the parents to find out how their children think and how they communicate. And the only way they can do this is to ask them. So, if you give a little educational sermon on death, I would suggest that you ask the kids questions on what you've just told them to make sure they've got it straight."

TEENAGERS

By the time children are in their teens, they probably understand just as well as adults what happens when a person dies. Their cognitive skills are developed, and unlike the younger child, they see death as something universal, inevitable, and irreversible. Acutely aware of themselves as people, teenagers may spend a lot of time philosophizing, criticizing, and daydreaming.

With puberty they watch their bodies change and mature, seeing the natural progression of the aging process that makes death possible. Death is a natural enemy to this new self who's emerging. If a person grows up to die, what's the sense of life? they ask.

With very young children, we have to spend a lot of time thinking about the words to use to help them understand about death. With a teen this usually isn't necessary. But what *is* necessary when they are confronted with death is to be there to help them through their grief, to understand their emotions, and to teach them how to act in this crisis. In this time of flux when they're shifting from being dependent to being independent, and experimenting with values and ways of behaving, teenagers need some firm and gentle guidance, someone to talk to. They are probably concerned about where they fit in at this time, what they're expected to do, and how to handle the myriad emotions that are brewing inside them. They may be feeling guilt, responsibility, and anger. "If only I had bugged Grandpa to take his medicine." "If only I had gone to see him in the hospital." They probably also have a heightened awareness of their parents' vulnerability. It all of a sudden hits them that nobody lives forever . . . how transient life is.

In her book *Peoplemaking*, Virginia Satir points out that parents teach in the toughest school in the world, the school of making people. In order to help them grow into kind, stable adults, we need to listen to them, talk with them, guide them. We have to treat them like people.

As we've seen, children are people with a special way of seeing the world. They have unusual ideas about death, and they are prone to certain misconceptions and difficulties with the subject at different ages. However, children can understand almost anything if it's put to them in the right way. You just have to know the right words to say. We'll talk more about this in the next chapter.

2.

Explaining Death to Children—
Crafting the Message

A six-year-old walked into the office of a funeral director in New Jersey, circled around the desk, and asked my colleague, "Mister, where are your wings?" The astonished man asked what the youngster meant and the child replied, "Well, Mommy said that an angel was coming to take Grandpa to heaven."

No one was trying to deceive that child. His mother was just giving him the best information she had at the time. The problem was that she hadn't packaged her message well, and on the way from parent to child the transmission was garbled. She hadn't used the right words to make the child understand what happens when a person dies.

Each family dealing with a death has a special set of circumstances unique to itself, depending on the individuals involved, their cultural traditions, religious outlooks, and what the children in the family know about death. All of these factors go into making up a sort of *family blueprint*, a way that each family has of doing things. No two family blueprints are the same, and in this book, no one explanation that I give will be exactly right for everyone, or will fit precisely into each family's blueprint. A family with a ninety-five-year-old aunt who has just died of old age won't have the same frame of reference as one in which a child died in an automobile accident. The family that has had to cope with two deaths in the last four years has a very different set of experiences than one that has never before experienced a death. There are no pat answers. What is right for Family A may not apply to Family B or C.

Look at your own family blueprint and see what it's made of. Who is the person who died? A distant relative, a grandparent you saw on weekends, or a member of the immediate family? How close that person was to the children will determine how deeply they will be affected.

I expect you to pick and choose from the information provided here. If you have a five-year-old, you may want to disregard the sections dealing with teenagers, taking only the information you need right now. First I'll talk about death close to home, in the family, then I'll discuss death outside the home—in the classroom, for example. Finally, we'll take a look at special situations that might come up—the death of an infant, accidental death, and the violent deaths of murder and suicide. In each case, I'll give you the specific words to use when telling your child that someone has died. In the Crisis Section at the back of this book, there is a fast, easy-to-refer-to outline of much of the information I will be presenting here. Turn to it when time is limited and you need to know what to say immediately.

DEATH OF A GRANDPARENT

Since the death of a grandparent is often one of the first encounters a child has with death, I'm going to go through this situation in some detail. It is the basic example to build on in other, more specialized, situations.

It's important to get to your child quickly, before friends and other relatives can, so that you can explain in your own way what has happened. Find a quiet place, and sit down; then, talking with the child as calmly and gently as possible, tell him what has happened. First, build the story: say that a very sad thing has happened—that Grandpa has died—and if necessary explain what "dead" means. Next, let him know that you'll be there to help him deal with this; that he's free to talk about how he feels; that he can ask questions and you'll try your best to answer them. I call this making a "communication contract." Finally, describe what will be happening over the next few days and where he fits in—tell him exactly what will happen to him. Children need to be told a beginning, a middle, and an end to their stories. Step by step, slowly, give your child the facts in words he or she will understand.

Here's what you might say to a five-year-old whose grandfather has died of old age. "A very, very sad thing happened to Grandpa. He was very, very, very old, so old that his body wore out and stopped working. Sometimes when a person is as old as Grandpa was, his body doesn't get better like ours do when it gets sick. It's not as strong as ours are. So it stops working and the person dies, and it can't be fixed anymore. That's what happened to Grandpa. That's why everyone is so sad."

Explain that "dead" means the body stopped working and won't do any of the things it used to do. It won't talk, walk, move, see, hear, think. It can't feel anything—it's no longer happy or sad or afraid; it can't feel heat, or cold, or pain. None of the parts of the body work anymore. It can't swallow or go to the bathroom. With a young child you might compare it to the time the goldfish died. (Using flowers or Mr. Hooper from "Sesame Street" as a comparison might be tricky; flowers reappear in the spring and Mr. Hooper comes back in reruns.)

If the person has died from a disease, there are two ways to handle the message to the child, depending on whether the illness was prolonged or sudden. For a prolonged illness, where death has been a process, the child will, I hope, have been informed about the progress of the illness. You might say, "A very sad thing has happened. . . . Usually when people get sick, they get better. But sometimes they get sicker and sicker, and become so weak that their bodies can't fight the sickness anymore, like yours and mine can. And the body wears out and stops working and they die. That's what happened to Grandpa."

Perhaps the illness was a sudden one, like meningitis. "A terrible thing has happened and we are all very sad." (Describe what happened—heart attack, high fever, etc.) "The sickness was so strong and so bad that it wore down his body very fast and he couldn't fight it anymore, so he died. This doesn't happen very often. He didn't know he was going to die and neither did we, so we're surprised and upset."

Tell your child just the basics the first time you sit down together. Tell him only what he needs to know at that moment—that Grandpa is dead; what he died of; and what dead means.

It may be that the child will be stunned, unable to do anything but cry. Right now he's probably not interested in a detailed explanation. Later, he'll have questions, and if you leave the door open, he'll feel free to come and ask them.

Human beings seek out only the information they need at a given time.

If possible, tell each child in the family separately, or at least talk to the older ones privately and then the younger ones, making sure that each understands what "dead" means.

Maybe you have great difficulty talking about death. (Maybe it's not just difficult, it's almost impossible for you.) If so, tell your child frankly, "I had a tough time when my grandmother died when I was a kid, and I've never been able to talk about death. But I really think it's important, so I'm going to try it with you." Saying something like this will help put your reaction in perspective for the child—for a moment he or she gets a glimpse of the situation through your eyes. It helps open the lines of communication.

Avoid Euphemisms

As you're talking with your child, avoid euphemisms. Use words like *dead, stopped working,* and *wore out*—simple words to establish the fact that the body is biologically dead. (Later on, after the child understands that the person is dead forever, you might talk about an afterlife, if this is what you believe.)

Dead is a difficult word for some people to say, and many of us go to great lengths to avoid it. When we kill animals, we "put them to sleep." When a person has died, they've "gone away," "passed on," "left us," "checked out." When we adults hear that kind of talk, we can put it in context and decipher the message. We know what the person is saying. A child very often doesn't. Those words don't mean the same thing to a child that they do to an adult. They imply that the dead person willfully abandoned us or that he's trying to find his way back. A child who hears "she lost her father" imagines that maybe he'll be found sometime, maybe he'll come home again. "Gone away" implies a trip, like the time Grandpa went fishing in Vermont. He came back then; maybe he will this time.

Repeating conventional or religious concepts like "He's gone to heaven and he'll live forever" when you're mourning a person who's dead can be very confusing to a youngster. It gives him a mixed message: how can Grandpa be lying in the funeral home, dead, and be up in heaven at the same time? How come Mommy's so upset if Grandpa's going to "live forever"? I'm not suggesting that these concepts be avoided—just that care must be taken to ensure that the child understands the fact of death as well.

One woman I know whose favorite aunt died when she was nine remembers sitting in the church and listening carefully as the minister gave the eulogy describing death as a passing of the seasons. Through the winter, she waited patiently for the spring to come, expecting her aunt to come back with the flowers. She was understandably very upset when the aunt didn't reappear.

Another word to avoid when you're talking with children about death is the word *sleep*, as one mother I talked with found out.

> "Have you said anything yet to Jennifer about your father?"
> "Yes. She knows he's not with us anymore."
> "She's four years old now?"
> "Right."
> "What did you say?"
> "Well, when we first came into your office before my father died she wanted to know why he wasn't here, because she expected to see him. I told her he was in the hospital and he was very sick and he wasn't waking up anymore. She asked why we can't wake him up, and I said he's so sick he's in a very deep sleep, and he may die. And she asked me why and

I said, 'because God doesn't want him to be hurting anymore.' And she cried for awhile."

I advised that mother to get back to her daughter as quickly
as she could and reverse what she had said about sleeping. Her
grandfather was definitely not sleeping. When you're sleeping, your eyes are closed but your body still works. When
someone is in a coma, his body doesn't work by itself, and
when a person dies, it stops working altogether. Some people
who are dead look like they're sleeping, but they're not—
they're dead. You don't want the child to think that dead is
sleeping, because what happens when Daddy or Jennifer goes
to sleep? She'd be afraid that she'd fall asleep, wake up alone,
and find that she's buried in the ground.

Another thing to remember when you're talking with children is that God doesn't kill people. Nor does God go around
zapping them because He wants them to be in heaven with
Him . . . like some sort of crazed social director in the sky.
Death comes from within the person; the body wears out and
dies. After you've explained that the person is biologically
dead and buried in the cemetery, then you can tell her about
God and an afterlife, if you choose.

Showing Emotion

Right from the beginning, let your child know that showing
emotion is okay. Explain that this is a very, very sad time and
that everyone is upset and that many of us may be crying—
even Mommy and Daddy. That's because we're sad that we
won't see the person anymore because he died. Crying is
normal; that's what we feel like doing sometimes when a
person dies. You should also explain that many people do
not show emotion openly when they're upset, but that doesn't
mean they didn't love the dead person. If we explain the

emotional turmoil that the child feels all around him, he won't be frightened by the change that he sees in us and in others. He'll understand that people may be acting differently than they usually do and he'll see why this is so.

This is an especially important concept to get across to older children. As I've already said, with teenagers you probably won't have to worry about their understanding of death; what they'll need is the facts, and your emotional support and understanding. Without being patronizing, make sure the child understands what you're saying. Remember that he or she may be in shock.

Anna and her husband have two children, aged twelve and thirteen. Their grandfather died of a stroke. He hadn't really been sick, just a little high blood pressure and things of that nature. Then he had a massive stroke. It was a sudden shock for everybody, and there were a lot of feelings bouncing around. I suggested that they say to their children, "Look, if you feel upset about something, talk to us about it."

If you feel upset, too, it's a good idea to talk about it. Many of the parents who've used my program say that sharing their feelings with their children works very well—it helps the children know that what *they're* feeling is okay.

All of this is part of the "communication contract" that you make with your child. Say to the youngster, "Listen, we're not going to hide anything from you. We'll probably all be upset at times and if we feel like crying, that's okay. Sometimes I'll need help. Sometimes we'll talk about Grandpa and the things we remember about him. We're all part of a family and we'll get through this together."

Explain What Happens Next

After you've gotten across the fact that the person is dead, and you've made your communication contract, the next step is to explain what's going to happen next. Here's what I might say to a little one if I were explaining a traditional Christian funeral.

"Grandpa is going to be moved from the hospital to the funeral home. That's a place where we'll keep Grandpa until the day of the funeral. We have to go to the funeral home soon and speak to the man there about the funeral plans. We'll tell him what clothes we want him to put on Grandpa, and we'll pick out a casket. That's a box we put Grandpa in so that when he gets buried no dirt will get on him [this is important to many children]. Grandpa will be at the funeral home for two days, so that people can come and say prayers and tell everyone how sorry they are. Then we take Grandpa to church, where we'll have a funeral and the priest (minister) will say more prayers. After church we'll go to the cemetery. Grandpa and Grandma picked out a special place there called a grave, and that's where we'll bury Grandpa. Then we put a stone on top of the grave with his name on it. It's a place we can visit and put down some flowers and say a prayer."

For a Jewish service, I would say this:

"Grandpa is being taken to the funeral home, where we will be able to be with him tomorrow. He will be dressed all in white, and will wear the talis we gave him. He will be in a casket made of wood. Our family and friends will come to be with us. The rabbi will speak about Grandpa and will pray for him. We will take Grandpa to the cemetery, where he will be placed in the ground. Later on, we'll go back for a visit, and you will be able to place a small stone there as a remembrance of Grandpa. After we return from the cemetery, our relatives and friends will come to visit with us and sit shiva. Daddy and Grandma will both be sitting on boxes [if that is the case]. We will have a candle burning for Grandpa, to remind us how much we loved him and how much we will miss him."

As time goes on, some children will require more explanation, depending on how affected they are by the death. Once the dialogue with your child has been started, though, it should not be too difficult to pick it up again.

Outlining the next few days—where you'll be, where they'll be, and what you'll all be doing—will save them a lot of anxiety. If they can't be with you, knowing what you'll be doing and when you'll be back will ease their minds. The integrity of the family has been shaken and they probably feel insecure. Children like to know where things stand, what to expect, who will take care of them, and where they fit in, and they have a right to know these things.

To a very young one, say something like: "I'm going to the funeral home now and I'll be back at two." Then, pointing to the clock, "That's when the little hand of the clock is right here. Aunt Dot will fix lunch for you and she'll take you to the playground. . . ." And so on, making sure that there are no surprises for the child. Blocking out the time for them will give them a framework to help them adjust in this time of upheaval.

Questions to Expect

Once you've given your child the information, and gently made sure that he or she has understood what you've said, you can anticipate a variety of questions, which can come right away or several days later. There are several different kinds of questions you can expect to get; they may be asked directly or indirectly.

When is he coming back?   First, with the very young child, you'll be asked questions relating to the functioning of the body. The little one who doesn't want to believe that death is final is hoping that at some point you'll give him a "yes" answer, which would mean the body is working again.

Is Grandpa cold in the ground? Is he lonesome, hungry, afraid? When will he be coming home? Hasn't he been dead long enough? Your answer to all these questions is that, "No, he's not lonesome, hungry, cold, etc., because in order to be those things the body has to be working. And Grandpa's body isn't working anymore. He's dead and he won't be coming home anymore . . . ever." Remember to tell your child that this is not like what he sees on TV. The cartoons he watches are make-believe; this is real. Grandpa won't be getting up again. That's why we're so sad; he's dead forever.

"Forever" is a tough concept for anyone to comprehend, but for a child it's really difficult. Tell him you're going to take him to the movies on Friday and he'll say, "Friday! That's such a long time!" His time is marked by the mileposts in his life—Christmas, his birthday, when he starts school. From September to December can seem like an eternity. He just doesn't understand "forever."

How old are you? This is another of the basic questions that will turn up in different forms. One father at first didn't buy the ideas I've been outlining here; he told me that his six-year-old was taking it all very well, that he understood what "dead" means and that he wasn't in the least bit concerned about his grandmother's death. A couple of days after the funeral the child spent quite a bit of time with a pencil and paper, writing down and adding up numbers. Later, while his mother was giving him a bath, he made a remark that caused his father to reverse his position about talking to children about death. "I've been doing some adding and I've figured out how old you are, Mommy," the child proclaimed. "And Daddy, too! You're seventy-three and he's eighty-seven." That child certainly calculated wrong—his father was in his early 30's! But behind that child's observation was the fear of his parents' death. Remember, age and death are connected in a child's mind. He has little understanding of the degrees of time or age, or how old is *old*. In the mind of a little one, babies are "newer," a teenager is older, and everyone over twenty, including his parents, is really long in the tooth. What you have to do is make him understand that Grandpa was so old he was two times as old as Daddy and Mommy.

Here's an answer to the "Are you going to die, too?" questions related to the question of age: "Everyone dies sometime. But I don't expect to die until you are very old and have children of your own. Once in a while people get very sick or get in a very bad accident; then they die before they're very, very old. But most of the time people don't die until they're very, very, *very* old."

"Why did he have to die? Why couldn't he get better?"   The third basic question that your youngsters may ask has to do with why the person died, and why he couldn't be cured. It's not enough to say, "Grandpa got a pain in his stomach and died." A child's mind might handle that information this way: "I had a tummy ache last week and I felt sick. Maybe I'm going to die now." Because he draws from his own experience, a child's knowledge is limited. So you have to work to get across how sick Grandpa really was . . . so sick that the child has never experienced anything like it. As we've seen, a young child takes things literally and connects things that don't belong together. He may hear someone say, "Boy, that flu really got to me. I was so sick I could have died!" Assure the youngster that Grandpa's sickness was different from the times each of you get sick. "Grandpa was very, very, very, very sick. Not sick like you feel when you get a tummy ache. Not sick like Daddy gets when he gets a headache. Not sick like Mommy when she gets a cough."

There was something wrong with the way Grandpa's body was working. Explain that your bodies are normal, and that when you get sick your bodies are strong enough to fight the sickness and make it go away. Grandpa's body couldn't do that. Some things can't be fixed. So he died.

"Did I do it?" A final question children often ask has to do with responsibility. Couldn't somebody have saved him? Couldn't it have been someone else? Explain that sometimes bad things happen in this world. Since everyone in the world has to die sometime, the people who love them are going to be sad and miss them just like we miss Grandpa. There's nothing anyone could have done. No one caused Grandpa to die (unless there were special circumstances, which we'll discuss later on). Add that sometimes children feel that they said or did something that caused Grandpa to die, but that's just not so. People die because their bodies stopped working.

The "I did it" syndrome, or misdirected thinking, isn't confined just to the minds of children. How often we adults blame ourselves for the death of a loved one! "If only I had gotten him to the hospital on time." "If only I had tried harder to get him to stop smoking." As children get older, they often have these reactions, common to grieving adults. The clue to their thinking might be questions like, "Couldn't the doctors have given him just one more blood transfusion?"— or a statement such as, "If only I had called the ambulance faster." What the child may really be asking is, "Am I in any way responsible for this? Is there any way I could have prevented it?" Your answer to him or her is "No." Taking a logical look at the facts, you explain that there's nothing he or she could have done.

As children get older, many of their questions will have to do with changing relationships. Who will take care of Grandma now that Grandpa is dead? How is this going to affect our family? What about me? Who's going to read me stories now that he is dead? Underneath these questions are feelings of insecurity and unrest. By giving your child the facts, letting him know what to expect, and making him a part of the group, you'll ease a lot of those fears.

Over the days and weeks following a death, children may ask and re-ask these basic questions again and again in slightly different ways. If they ask something that you can't answer, be honest and say you don't know. It's better to admit that you don't understand something than to fill a child's mind with a deception or half-truth. Tell him that death is a tough subject, a mystery, and that you don't know everything. But don't let that be a cop-out, either. Children deserve answers to their questions, given on a level that they'll understand. If you can't explain something, find someone who can. If you're very disturbed at the time your child asks a question, hug him or her and say, "I can't talk about it now, I'm too upset. We'll talk about it later." But follow through on your promise, so the child doesn't feel put off.

Trying to cover every eventuality, making sure that every question is anticipated, is, of course, an impossible task. What we aim for is to be sensitive and open to our children. As you listen to their questions, you'll find out more about what they are thinking. One mother told her four-year-old only that Grandpa had died and gone to heaven. As they walked in the door of the funeral home, the mother was stopped in her tracks by the child's question, "Is this heaven?" The mother knew she'd have to back-track and explain what was what. "I realized at that point that what I had been saying to her was not correct."

The Question of an Afterlife

Each family has to handle the question of an afterlife in its own way, and sometimes the views of your friends and relatives will differ from your own. Try to get across what you believe as quickly as possible, so that your child will have a firm foundation before others have their say.

Sometimes well-meaning relatives, sharing their religious beliefs in an attempt to comfort the child, can cause a great deal of concern. Take the statement, "God loved Grandpa, and He took him to heaven." What seems like a valid if simply stated religious belief can give the child a very different message: "God loves Mommy and Daddy and me, too. Maybe we'll all be taken away like Grandpa."

I am in no way discounting the importance of religious conviction, but faith involves believing what you cannot see, trusting, and being willing to wait for the answer, and it's a tough thing for many children. It's a wonderful gift, and people who have faith often are much better able to deal with their grief and feelings of loss than those who don't. Children who have been prepared with a good biological explanation of why the person died may then be ready for the explanation of what happens after life. Religion can be a beautiful ending to the story of what happened to Grandpa. But problems occur when people use it as a beginning, middle, and end to the story, without saying anything else.

DEATH OF AN IMMEDIATE FAMILY MEMBER (MOTHER, FATHER, SIBLING)

According to a report issued in 1984 by the National Academy of Sciences, the children most deeply affected by a death in their immediate family are usually young children who have lost their mothers, or teenagers whose fathers have died.

But any child who has had death hit so close to home usually has a very difficult time.

Dolores Callahan, describing her family's experience in an article in *Thanatos*, a publication on bereavement, pointed out that in a family we interact by drawing from and contributing to each other's lives. When her sister died, "all of a sudden a piece of the pie was missing." Not only did the family lose the sister and her unique personality, but the family design was ripped apart, its wholeness shattered, and because of that each of the members felt diminished. "It's hard to accept. We felt disfigured by her loss."

Children are not supposed to die. They're expected to live long, productive lives and grow into old age. So when a child dies, the parents sometimes feel so disturbed and helpless that for a while they can't maintain a healthy relationship with their other children or with each other. Three-quarters of the couples who experience the death of a child separate or divorce. The family is thrown into crisis. Parents sometimes expect one of the other siblings to take the place of the dead child, and sometimes they retreat into themselves, shutting out the other children. That can be very harmful to a child, who learns how to grieve by watching his or her parents.

"What was it like for my parents when Gene died?" asks Claudia Typond in *The Death of a Child—A Case Study*. "They surely went through some kind of hell, yet I never saw it. All that was visible was a wall of silence."

A child picks up on the anxiety that his parents are feeling, and it often feeds on his own fears. The sidekick he lived with and played with and fought with and laughed with is dead. Her bike is still in the garage. Her rock albums are still next to the stereo. She was part of the family's life, and yet she's not here anymore. "If it happened to my own sister, it can happen to me," he may be thinking. "Will it happen tomorrow or next week?" . . . "Mommy doesn't love me anymore. She's always crying even though it's been such a long time since Jimmy died. She probably wishes I had died instead." Young children may also lose some of their confidence in their parents' ability to protect them from harm.

These are some of the thoughts that may be milling around in the child's mind, and his behavior may well reflect his distress. Matthew wanted to make everything right in the family again. Although not a very athletic fellow, he took up football, trying to fill the slot his brother, "the jock," had left. Confused and angry, six-year-old Steven refused to do his schoolwork, sitting passively in the corner while the rest of the class worked around him. He just didn't know what to say.

The situation can be even worse for a child when the parent dies. Irwin was a teenager, very busy juggling school and work, but nearly every bit of extra time he had was spent at the hospital, next to the bedside of his sick father. One evening Irwin took a break, went out for dinner with a friend, then went racing back to the hospital room to spend the rest of the evening with his dad. "My father was gone. The mattress was rolled up on the bed," Irwin says. "I'll never forget that scene. I never got a chance to tell him goodbye." And yet, if you had met Irwin that evening, you would never have known he was that deeply upset.

Children grieve differently from adults. Instead of experiencing intense distress, many children are likely at first to deny the death, then grieve intermittently for many years. Researchers point out that because of this, they can suffer emotional disturbances that carry over into adulthood.

In her book *How It Feels When a Parent Dies*, Jill Krementz talked with eight youngsters ranging in age from seven to sixteen. One child whose grief was more immediately apparent told her, "When Mom told me that Daddy was dead, my knees started shaking. I almost fell down. My sister Peg screamed when she found out. My hands still shake when I think about my father." Another was plagued with nightmares. "I had a dream that she was lying at the bottom of a closet and she came back to life. When I have dreams like that, I just pinch myself on the arm to see if I'm awake or dreaming."

Nightmares are not uncommon when a close family member dies. Since it's awfully hard to break the spiritual connection with someone who has been so close to you, other family members may hear the dead person laugh or cry, or may imagine that he appears to them in a mystical experience. Paul Patterson of the Albany Medical College said that these experiences are often strikingly similar to the grief-induced hallucinations that occur during the transfer from sleep to awakening in the morning. Just as people are coming out of their dreams, "when our unconscious is most susceptible to control . . . our minds produce the phenomenon of the spirit hovering over the body."

What do you say to children when someone so close to them dies unexpectedly? When a brother or sister they grew up with, or a parent they idolized, is suddenly dead, and the family seems to be shattered? Perhaps you might explain it to a child around the age of five in this way. (Of course, you'll also want to add some of the basic information, such as what "dead" means, which we discussed in the section on the death of a grandparent.)

"Sometimes terrible things happen to us in life, and something terrible has happened to our family. Your brother Jimmy has died. He got very, very, very sick with a disease not many people get, and he died very fast. It's nobody's fault because no one could have saved him. There are some things we just can't understand. We'll miss Jimmy awfully because he won't be seeing him again, and we loved him, and he loved us very much. But even without Jimmy we'll still always be a family, and we'll stick together."

If you have older children, you'll have to tailor the explanation to fit their needs. As I pointed out in the last chapter, preteens will probably be interested in the technical details of how the death occurred, for example, while a nine-year-old would need to be reassured that death is not contagious. Above all, don't adhere rigidly to my suggestions for the level of information needed by different age groups. You know your children better than anyone else does; use this material only as a guide.

When one parent dies, another issue that almost always comes up is concern about the other parent. "What will happen to me if you also die?" the child wonders. Be prepared to answer this question honestly and reassuringly.

The way in which children work through their grief depends a lot on how their parents and the other members of their family handle themselves, and whether or not the other family members reach out to them. The stronger the state of the helping adult, the better for the child. If the adult encourages the child to grieve, lets him know how much the dead person loved him and what joy the child brought to him, the youngster will be better able to cope. Also, if life is kept relatively stable, it will make things a lot easier for the child.

This sense of stability is not an easy thing for parents to maintain. Since a death in the immediate family is such a blow, some parents are not able to cope with the death themselves, much less help their kids. Elise Longpré, whose husband died in a car crash, advises grieving families not to be afraid to go for help. She contacted MADD, Mothers Against Drunk Drivers, a victim support group. "I had been independent till now and it never crossed my mind to accept any help," she wrote in *Thanatos*. "In fact, I would refuse when someone offered their help." But she decided that she had to change. "I found myself accepting help and each time it became easier. Because of this, I am mingling more with people now." There are a number of other support groups, such as Compassionate Friends, that help families in crisis; I've listed some of them in the back of this book. Very often, however, a family will need the help of a trained professional to make it through the grief.

A few final suggestions on dealing with the death of a family member:

① First, let the children know who would take care of them if you died, and to whom they should go for help in an emergency. They think about such things; they'll feel more secure if they know what to expect.

② Second, let the family be together in the ritual of grieving. If a child's brother has died, for example, let him put his brother's special toys in the casket beside him. Older children can be pallbearers; younger ones can put flowers on the altar.

③ Finally, as the family grieves, help each member find some kind of identification with the dead person. One young boy constantly wore his dead brother's high-school letter jacket, even though it swallowed him up. A fourteen-year-old girl helped her father finish stripping a table the mother had been working on. In the next chapter, I'll talk about the processes of grief and healing in more detail.

Can anything good come out of the death of someone we love? At first you think absolutely not. But sometimes when we are confronted with loss, the grieving we go through can help us find more direction in our lives. As people suffer, they often become more open to others and in the crisis start sharing their feelings and thoughts with other members of their family, after years of keeping things to themselves. A crisis sometimes brings out the best in people. "After this, I know I can handle anything," one mother said. "I know now that our family will stick together and who our friends are.

What living is is having other people. When Joe died, it was those other people who helped us get through. Lovely, lovely people. Thank God we had our friends."

If a Member of Your Family is Dying

Very often when I sit down with a family to make funeral arrangements, I begin by asking if the children knew this person was sick. The parents will often say that yes, they knew he was sick but they didn't know that he was dying. Then, when the person dies, the children are very often shocked. "She might just as well have been hit by a bus," one young man remarked. "We had no idea she was going to die."

When a loved one is dying, the others in the family experience "anticipatory grief," according to Dr. Paul Patterson. Even before the death occurs, since they know it's coming, the adults already begin to mourn for the person. Children pick up on that grief. Dr. Patterson advises parents to be honest with their children about the dying person's chances of survival. If the odds are only ten percent, say so.

During the final months and days before a death, the demands on the parents are enormous. Overwhelmed with their own feelings of grief, they sometimes withdraw from their children; this can be highly upsetting to the youngsters, who are anxious about being abandoned. When the family does stay united in its attempt to cope with grief—when all the family members understand what was going on, and the children are involved and can help out a bit—everyone benefits from the experience.

INFANT DEATH

When a newborn baby dies it's the closest thing to insanity most parents could ever imagine. I know—my first-born son, Daniel, died when he was not yet a day old.

In those days, twenty years ago, when a baby was born dead or died shortly after birth, it was thought that the best thing to do was to quietly bury the child with no wake or funeral, so Daniel was taken directly to the cemetery. My wife, Barbara, never saw her first son. Although she very much wanted to see him, I wouldn't let her. There was no question in my mind that I was doing the right thing. I had talked to our relatives about what you do in a situation like this and they explained the way it was handled. The hospital people, the priest, the family . . . everyone agreed that I should spare her the pain of seeing her dead child. "Get it over with so she'll forget about it," they said.

I went along with what other people said, against the wishes of my wife, doing what I felt was right, what I thought was best for her . . . trying to help her block it out of her mind. It wasn't until some years later, when Barbara and I began discussing our feelings about Daniel, that I saw how I had been trying to make believe the child had never existed. I had so thoroughly pushed the experience out of my mind that when I was first working on this chapter, I couldn't even remember in what month the baby had been born.

Barbara wasn't able to block out Daniel as effectively as I was. When a baby dies, a parent—especially the mother—never forgets, never really stops the grieving. Sure, the pain lessens over time, but it's impossible to eradicate it. Tina Russo Quirk, a nurse writing about infant death in the *Journal of Nurse-Midwifery*, called it "one of the loneliest of losses," with no wake, no flowers, no memories to share.

Another complication that aggravates the grieving process

is one involving self-image. Often, when a newborn dies the parents feel that they were somehow responsible, that something must have been wrong with them physically, causing them to produce a defective child. This feeling of guilt can be especially strong if Sudden Infant Death Syndrome is the cause of the baby's death (we'll discuss this in more detail shortly). Absorbed in their grief and shame, parents sometimes blame each other, the doctors, and God. These desperate feelings are naturally picked up by the other children in the family.

Relating to and Helping the Other Children

In an article published in *Pediatrics Magazine*, Barbara Elliott, a nurse whose twin sons died when they were just a week old, talked about how tough it was for her and her husband to relate to their other children, ages two and four. "The two-year-old kept repeating, 'Babies out of tummy, babies dead. No more babies.' The four-year-old understood our sadness and knew the babies were never coming home." Mrs. Elliott said that after a series of bad days at home, the four-year-old returned to preschool and that seemed to help. But she still had a hard time caring for her youngsters. "I was so wrapped up in my own feelings that I could not see how much they needed me. I was intolerant of them. Then the two-year-old got the flu. As his fever rose, I kept thinking what it would be like if he died, too. Then I knew how much he needs me, and how much I needed him to love. I was jolted. I knew I had not been able to support or find joy in them."

"I've lost my ability to love. I just can't give anymore." That's how many parents whose newborns have died feel for awhile. It's hard to be patient with little children who are picking up the vibrations in the family that all is not well, and are acting up because of it.

Trying to help the other children come to terms with what has happened is the most difficult part of coping with the death. Cleveland psychologist Erna Furman, who has been working with bereaved children for thirty years, says, "Why is it so difficult? In part, it is because the feelings of the children about the newborn baby are so totally different from the parent's feelings. . . . To the children, and to young children in particular, this baby was not looked forward to as a cherished newcomer—it was a potential rival without whom they could have easily gotten along happily in life." Furman adds that the questions the child is likely to ask—"Can it happen to me and to you, Mommy?", or "Was it your fault, Mommy, or was it my fault?"—are especially difficult for the parent to answer.

To explain to the children why a baby has been born dead or has lived for just a few hours, a parent can say the following: "Sometimes when a new baby is born, it's very, very sick, so sick that his body stops working and dies." Explain the cause of death, if you know it (that his lungs were not developed, for example). "It's nothing that anybody did or forgot to do. Doctors are not sure why it happens, but with our little baby, his body didn't grow correctly and all of his parts inside were not working right, so he died."

St. John's Hospital in Springfield, Illinois, offers a list of suggestions for helping families who have lost a newborn child:

- Name the child. This helps to include the baby in the family's life and helps recognize the child's existence.
- Keep a memory book, a tangible record of the family's feelings during the time of loss.
- Have a picture taken of the baby and dispose of the baby's things yourselves. That acknowledges that the baby lived and died.

- A birth certificate with footprints should be made up. Both parents should be involved in the decision of whether or not there should be an autopsy, and both parents should also decide on the burial plans. These joint decisions help promote family communication.
- Each parent should decide if he or she wants to hold the dead baby.

Most parents I've talked to said they benefited from seeing their dead baby. Even in cases where the child was born badly deformed, parents have tended to look at the normal parts of the child, saying things like, "Well, all his toes are there and his fingers are fine." Seeing the baby often helps parents to better accept the death.

Should a dead child's brothers and sisters be allowed to attend the funeral? Furman suggests that adolescents should be allowed to decide for themselves; younger children, if they are accompanied by their parents, are also usually helped by attending the funeral. Most experts agree that it's really up to the individual family.

Sudden Infant Death Syndrome

One of the most traumatic things that can happen to a family is to have a baby die from Sudden Infant Death Syndrome, or SIDS. Apparently healthy one minute, then dead the next, the child just all of a sudden stops breathing. Unexpected and so far unexplained, SIDS is the cause of seven thousand deaths a year,* usually in the children's first year, leaving their families shocked and disbelieving, and having to cope with denial, anger, and depression.

---

*According to Christine Blenninger, project coordinator for the New York City Information and Counseling Program for Sudden Infant Death.

Today, with the new public awareness of child abuse, the parent whose child has been a victim of SIDS often ends up defensively explaining that the death was not caused by anything he did or did not do. For many, it's not a sufficient explanation. "What do you mean, you don't know what the baby died of?" In this age when medical science has answers for everything, the fact that there's no answer for SIDS is incomprehensible to some people. If the baby died of some disease that people had heard of, there'd be no further need to explain, no need for more questions. But most of the time with SIDS, they don't understand.

Because of the senselessness of SIDS, because the parents have such a hard time coming to grips with it, this type of death is especially hard to explain to the other children in the family. Here are a few words, necessarily very simple, that you can say to a little child whose brother or sister has died from SIDS.

> "Sometimes with little babies something happens that makes their bodies stop working. It's hard to explain because no one's sure what it is, but that's what happens sometimes. It's nothing anyone did or forgot to do. It just happened."

Older children who need more of an explanation should be told what was *not* the cause of SIDS. Here's what the National SIDS Clearinghouse tells us: A SIDS death was not anyone's fault; not hereditary or contagious; not caused by external suffocation, by vomiting, or by choking. SIDS infants do not suffer when they die. It could not have been predicted or prevented by anyone. A medical reality that can be determined only by an autopsy, SIDS can strike any family, rapidly and silently, usually during periods of sleep.

Emphasize to the children that SIDS kills infants, not older children, so they won't be afraid that they will die when they go to sleep. Finally, let the child know that it's happened to many other babies as well—it's the major cause of death in the period after the first month until the end of the first year.

In a study at the Children's Hospital in Boston on the effect of a SIDS death on the other siblings in the family, the authors found that the trauma greatly affected the children; there were changes in the behavior patterns of eighty percent of the children they studied. Because of SIDS, the family structure was abruptly altered. Big brother and big sister roles were suddenly terminated in a catastrophic manner, and the children were knocked off-balance for awhile. Some of the youngsters regressed in their toilet training and some had trouble eating; others had problems interacting with their playmates, and most had trouble sleeping. Unable to understand what had happened to their apparently healthy brother or sister, they were confused, disrupted, and afraid of going to bed at night. In the Boston study, one three-year-old described her nightmare: a monster was coming to take her because she had killed her baby brother. A second child dreamed that a monster was coming to take her to heaven to be with her brother. Another child had night terrors, frightening episodes where in the middle of the night the youngster started screaming. Her mother understood: "She was right here when it happened [when the baby died], and I was screaming. She wakes up screaming now. I have to lie down with her to get her to go back to sleep."

Some of the SIDS parents in the study, not knowing which way to turn, spoiled their other children in their need to be close to them. "Holding him brought me comfort that no one else could. I had to know that he was safe and I could only know that by holding onto him." Others distanced themselves from their children for awhile. "I couldn't stand to be near her. I was afraid of what would happen."

Sometimes the confused children lashed out, but sometimes they reassured their parents. "It's okay," said one little child, talking about his dead brother. "He's in heaven with the angels." Another told her mother, "Don't be too sad, you still have me." One mother said that she didn't know who needed more hugging, her child or herself.

Hugging. Sometimes that's about all you can do after you've told your child that his baby brother or sister has died. Hugging, and answering questions, and crying together. It will be a long time before your family will be able to make sense out of this . . . if you ever do. For a long time you'll be struggling with the feelings of guilt and grief and the question, "What happened?"

How this death is dealt with will have a lasting effect on your other children. It's probably the first time they've ever experienced a death, especially one so close to them, someone dear whom they watched grow bigger and helped take care of. Let your children share your grief. Accept their feelings, taking care not to work out your own grief through them.

When friends come to visit and offer their condolences, don't send your young one out of the room. He may think something terrible will happen again or that everyone is talking about him. He feels very insecure right now. He needs your support and your love . . . and to know you won't leave him. Open discussions, where he'll get the answers he needs, are a must for a family victimized by the death of an infant. By talking out their feelings, by helping them draw pictures or write down what's on their minds, they'll express how they feel and work out the grief.

Most parents and counseling professionals I've talked to said that once a child is old enough to understand what is going on, taking him to the funeral is a good idea. The ritual gives him a framework in which to start the grieving process. (See Chapter 4 for more about involving children in the funeral.)

DEATH OUTSIDE THE FAMILY (IN THE CLASSROOM)

When death occurs in the classroom, it can be almost as shattering to a youngster as if a close family member had died. That's because the teachers and classmates make up a kind of second family for the child. It is at school that children spend most of their day and much of their free time, so it's natural to be very upset if someone at school dies.

Francis De Bernardo in *The Tablet,* a Catholic newspaper in New York City, interviewed children who had watched their high school teacher collapse and die during chemistry class at Bishop Ford High School in Brooklyn. "One moment he was standing there and then he grabbed his chest . . . and fell to the floor," one child remembered. The students went into action, some of them aiding the dying teacher, others ushering their classmates, gasping and crying, out of the classroom.

For many of those teenagers, this was their first direct experience with death, and several months later when De Bernardo talked with them they were still trying hard to accept it. Among the questions they asked themselves was, "Why did it have to be our classroom?" Father Jim Devlin, assistant chaplain at the school, explained to them that it is very normal to feel angry because death is often so irrational. "There are some things that can't be explained away." Since their teacher's death was so sudden and hard to comprehend, many of the youngsters felt guilty, thinking that somehow they could have saved him. Others pushed it out of their minds. One boy said he tried to talk to his mother but he couldn't say anything. Another said he'd learned to appreciate people more, not to take them so much for granted. Suddenly aware of how quickly death can come, one child realized that life is a precious gift—and so are his parents. "I realized that . . . there's no age limit. I thought I should show them I love them more . . . get closer to them."

The Compassionate Friends Newsletter suggests that since the class functions as a group, the students might share grief as a class. The teacher might read a library book on death and grieving with the class; lead a classroom discussion; make a scrapbook; or plant a memorial tree. But most of all, say the Compassionate Friends, the teacher can be there to talk with.

One of the positive by-products of the tragic increase in teenage suicides in recent years has been the establishment of courses in death and dying in a number of high schools. In these courses, adolescents learn why some people choose to kill themselves, what the danger signals are for suicide, and how they can go to their teacher or another adult for help if they hear any of their friends talking about suicide, or are contemplating it themselves. Openness in talking about suicide, and about death in general, removes much of the mystique that can make it appealing to youngsters; it also helps break the chain reaction that can develop after one suicide occurs in a community.

The benefits of grieving together can extend to a whole community. In July 1979, six teenagers on their way to work in the cornfields near Sandwich, Illinois, were killed in a car crash. "Six of Sandwich's finest—its cheerleaders, the prom queen, track stars, choir girls—were dead. Instantly, with no preparation. No chance to say goodbye," wrote Barbara Snyder in the *Buffalo News* (N.Y.). Dr. Carol Troescher, a grief counselor originally from Buffalo, New York, was working in a town near Sandwich. She immediately contacted the Sandwich School Superintendent, asked what she could do to help, and ended up working in Sandwich for two years. As Dr. Troescher put it, the town was like a mosaic with six of its bright, colorful stones missing; she had to keep the mosaic from "becoming unglued."

She sat around kitchen tables and looked at photo albums as the families talked about the girls they lost. "There's Paula on the track team. . . . She was stubborn . . . had a great sense of humor." They needed to reminisce about their loss. Sometimes the kids had to remind their parents not to focus all their attention on their dead sisters. Finally, as the months and years passed—after they had said, "That's enough"—the people of Sandwich began to heal. Dr. Troescher explained, "They realized there was nothing they could do. They asked, 'What is this going to do to our lives? Is this going to kill us? Is this going to break us apart? Or are we going to go on living?' " Some families were torn apart; other families pulled together.

Dr. Troescher conducted classes on dealing with grief at the high school; she brought in speakers and invited the students to share their poetry and music that helped them through the calamity. But, reports Snyder, the most dramatic and tangible thing that came out of the tragedy at Sandwich was a booklet called "Thanks for the Memories," a collection of poems, stories, and sketches about the dead girls, done by their friends and families . . . the reminiscenses of a community that mourned, then pulled out of grief.

ACCIDENT

"Life," say Audrey Gordon and Dennis Klass in *They Need to Know*, "at times may be something to cry about." When death is a result of old age, or is a slow, gradual passing away, the family is given a little time to prepare for the inevitable. In the case of an accident, death comes as a terrific shock. The family feels victimized; something or someone has taken control of fate. A mother, talking with her friends in the park, looks away for a moment and her child runs into the street and is hit by a car.

When there's an accident, the family is often laden with anger and guilt. Mothers Against Drunk Drivers (MADD) have a right to be angry at those who drink and drive, and they're channeling their anger, making it quite productive. Undoubtedly lives will be saved by their efforts. But the guilt experienced by the child who accidentally broke his brother's neck while they were rough-housing is hard to channel. He feels responsible. That child may live for a lifetime with guilt unless he gets some professional help. People need to learn that sometimes bad things just happen, as Harold Kushner points out in his book *When Bad Things Happen To Good People*, and there's nothing anyone can do about it.

Children are usually able to comprehend death from an accident more easily than just about any other kind of death, because parents are always making such a big deal about how they should avoid them. "Don't go near the window. You might fall out." "Watch when you're crossing the street so you don't get hit by a car."

And so, when you're explaining a death caused by an accident, relate it back to something they've heard before: "You know how Mommy and Daddy are always telling you to be careful when you're crossing the street, because there are crazy drivers who could hit you? Well, a terrible thing has happened to Uncle Bill. . . ." Explain what happened in the accident. Go through the basic information about everybody being sad that the person is dead. Then explain why: "His body was hurt so badly that it couldn't be fixed, so it stopped working and he's dead."

MURDER

The headlines read, "Hero Cop Slain by Freak Shot in Siege." It was a warm September day and Susan was on her way out the door of her house, looking for her older son to take him for a haircut. "And all of a sudden, my neighbor drives up. He's with the town police. I could see from his face that something was wrong. 'Something's happened,' I said. 'Tell me right now, I know it's bad.' 'Joe's been shot,' the neighbor said. 'He didn't make it.'"

Susan didn't faint, she didn't go into hysterics. "Let me think for a moment," she said. "Please find my children." Within moments, fifteen policemen helicoptered into the little village, landed in the schoolyard nearby, then descended on her house. Without a word, they pushed past her through the door and combed the house. "My God, what's happening?" she said. Later, she was told that they were looking for a gun, afraid that Susan, in her grief, might kill herself.

What kind of effect will a scene like that have on the children in the family? In his work at New York's Harlem Hospital Center, Dr. Hal Fishkin has dealt with a number of youngsters whose parents have been murdered. "It's going to have a permanent impact on the child's life. Some children are resilient and can deal with it, but others, the vulnerable ones, need a particular sensitivity." Fishkin says that it's tough in a time of crisis for policemen, neighbors, and emergency room personnel to think about the children and about what's happening inside their minds—but it's necessary.

Fortunately, most children won't have to face what Susan's family did—the murder of someone close to them. But when it does happen, the child often experiences serious problems that may require professional help.

In an article in *Monitor*, a publication for psychologists, Carol Turkington quoted Alvin Pouissant of the Harvard

Medical School, who studied the reactions of children victimized by murder. "They felt violated—like rape victims—they wanted to seek revenge and hunt for the killer, and they exhibited terror of their environment."

Each child reacts differently. Jan lay in bed with a pair of pinking shears clutched in her hand for protection. Betsy couldn't go back into her house until the walls had been painted a different color, so the place wouldn't seem the same. Timothy, who watched as his mother was shot, dreams about killing the murderer.

Child psychologist Dr. Robert Pynoos of UCLA says that a child who's suffered through such a trauma will "hear that gunshot forever." Not only does the child have a horrible image to contend with, he is also plagued with the urge to pay the murderer back, so he imagines ways he'd execute him. This is especially traumatic if one parent killed the other. "The ambivalent urges to revenge the slain parent and to protect the remaining parent can never be satisfactorily resolved without some form of psychiatric treatment. . . . To see your parent killed is an event a child never recovers from."

What do you say to a child after someone he or she loves has been murdered? Begin by stating something along these lines: "Sometimes things happen in life—terrible things that we have no control over. Well, a terrible thing has happened." Explain that the person was murdered—shot or stabbed or whatever—and tell the child who did it: "A bad man we don't know . . .", "Uncle John went crazy and shot Daddy . . ."

Explain as simply as possible what happened, who did it, and why—if you know. Then try to help your child deal with the trauma. It's going to be tough if the person was a key figure in his social structure. If it was his mother or father, the death will have a profound effect on him, regardless of whether or not he was close to that parent or perhaps even hated him or her. His whole social system has been upset, and, as the late Harvard psychiatrist Erich Lindeman noted, the child needs to break the strong ties that he had to the dead person, to find other people to get close to.

When you're dealing with a murder, it's particularly important to involve the child in the funeral and the family's mourning process, to help the child stay in touch with reality. Also, as a way of softening the trauma, many experts suggest letting the child relive the experience, perhaps encouraging him or her to draw the scene of the murder in detail. Dr. Hal Fishkin says that when he's working with youngsters who have witnessed a death, whether it's a murder or an accident, he gets the child to relate all the details so he can find out what the child thinks happened. He compares these perceptions to what the police or other sources say actually happened. "You try to reconcile the two stories so you can know what the child is thinking," Fishkin advises. If the child describing the murder says, "He got mad at me and beat me," then the child may think it was his fault that the person got angry and killed his mother. "I might say something like, 'Well, your mother had terribly bad luck when she met him, because he's not a good man.' And you try to deal with the guilt and anger."

Eventually, as the months pass, new feelings will come out of the child. After six months, say Fishkin, the child will not be as enraged or depressed. "The big question is, do you allow the child to cover over and forget about it, or do you bring it up? That's a very hard thing to generalize. Different children need different things. With some, there's a turbulent, emotional response at the time of the trauma and you want to help them cover over . . . give them some support for their defenses. But with others—they're withdrawn and you know that there's a kind of precancerous growth inside that you have to excise in some way. You have to bring it out." In any case, therapy is almost always necessary to help the child deal with depression, desire for revenge, and loss of faith in the order of society.

SUICIDE

One of the most difficult kinds of death that a family ever has to cope with is one in which one family member feels directly responsible for the death of another. This is often the case with suicide. Prompted by hopelessness, despondency, or anxiety, the person who kills himself makes a statement to the world that he can't live anymore, and the survivors feel that he willfully abandoned them—that he didn't want to be around them anymore, that he didn't care what would happen. It's the ultimate rejection for those who are left.

Experts say that suicide is almost always the expression of a malfunction in the family system—an attempt to manipulate relationships in an inflexible family structure, or the revenge of a person who feels that no one cares and that he can no longer cope. UCLA researcher Dr. Edwin Shneidman says, "Psychodynamically, suicide can be seen as murder in the 180th degree."

Because of this, suicide leaves the family members permanently changed. It's an act that breeds turmoil and self-doubt as the bereaved try to understand it, all the while punishing themselves with recriminations. Because of the stigma attached to suicide, some people attempt to run away from the reality of it, making the situation even worse for any children in the family.

John Brogan and Ula Maiden teach a death and dying course to seventh- and eighth-graders in Yorktown Heights,

New York. Several years ago, they noticed that one of their students, Cindy, was very obviously depressed. One day, Cindy ran into their classroom, agitated; she pushed by Ula, gave her pocketbook to a friend, then went running down the hall. John took off after her, grabbed her, and saw that she had tried to cut her wrists. In her pocketbook were bottles of medicine that she had planned to take and a suicide note addressed to her friend. Hysterical, she was taken to the hospital and admitted to a psychiatric ward.

The students in that class watched the whole scene unfold. On the bus the next day, they naturally were talking about it. Also on the bus was Cindy's twelve-year-old brother, just one year younger than Cindy, who had no idea what everyone was talking about. When he found out that his sister had attempted suicide, he was shocked. Sure, he had noticed that his sister hadn't come home the night before, but his parents hadn't told him why. He had just assumed she was away at a friend's house.

When you're faced with a suicide attempt or an actual suicide, in which all questions of accident have been ruled out and people know what happened, refusing to talk about it with your children or to admit that it happened can be very traumatic for them. One boy came home after school and found his father lying in the living room with a gunshot wound in his head. His mother later told the child that his father had died of a heart attack. The child knew better; he would never forget that horrendous scene. Lying or withholding the truth destroys the child's not-fully-developed trust in those around him, and contributes to the chaotic atmosphere charged with stigma, guilt, anger, and betrayal. It's far better to have a loved one tell him the truth, in a simple but honest way, than to have to hear about it outside the home, where people might not be so kind. It's not a question of whether or not to tell the children, but rather how to tell them, when, and what to say.

Of course, coping with suicide involves more than simply talking out your feelings. In almost all cases, experts agree that the family should have professional help. Because suicide has an impact different from any other kind of death, there are all sorts of psychological complications—such as the fact that suicides sometimes repeat in a family—that should be dealt with by experienced counselors. Before talking with your child about a suicide, it's a good idea to consult a professional. After you have done so, here are some suggestions as to how you can open the lines of communication with your child.

① First of all, the experts I've talked to stress that it's important to find out exactly what happened before talking with the child. If you're sure the suicide was intentional—when there is no doubt that the person planned to kill him or herself—you might say: "Sometimes a person's body gets sick and doesn't work right. Sometimes a person's mind doesn't work right. He can't see things clearly and he feels the only way to solve this problem is by ending his life. That's what happened here. . . ."

② If you're not sure the death was actually a suicide—if the death was due to something like a drug or alcohol overdose—you might say, "Sometimes people take pills to relax, or to get to sleep, or to try to block out their problems. These pills make a person's body slow down, but too many make the body stop working. We don't know that he wanted to die, but that's what happened." To an older child you might add more information: "He had a very serious problem and he went through a period of weakness. If he had given himself time, he wouldn't have found it necessary to kill himself. This was the worst solution he could have chosen. But we have to try to understand him; he wasn't thinking clearly when he did it. You might be feeling angry with him—that it's unfair to you for him to have chosen this solution. That's okay; it's human to feel angry at a time like this."

Emotional Problems and Reactions

One of the feelings the child may be suffering from after a suicide is guilt. In one case, Andrew's father left a suicide note saying he couldn't go on living because he was so upset about his son's involvement with drugs. Naturally, the boy was left with the overwhelming sense that he was responsible for his father's death. "Look, this is really tough," psychiatrist Hal Fishkin told him, "but you weren't the only stressor in your father's life. He was unraveling, and the final part of his unraveling was his killing himself. It must be hard for you. If I were in your shoes, I'd feel awful."

When you're dealing with that kind of guilt, all of the experts agree that it's extremely important to let the child know that if a person really wanted to kill himself, there's nothing anyone could have done to stop him; somehow he would have found a way. "But if only I had picked up on the signs that he was going to do this!" the child is probably thinking. "If only I had been there I could have stopped him!" Let him know that much of the time, those closest to a suicide are the most surprised. So often we hear, "She was the last person in the world I would have expected to do that."

Anger is another emotion that's naturally associated with death. A person usually feels angry when someone he loves dies. But with other kinds of death, the anger can be easily directed against something, vented outward. "That horrible cancer!" "Those dumb doctors!" "That insane murderer!" With suicide the anger is sometimes tougher to direct; it tends to bounce all over, at the dead person's friends, at the other members of the family, at the psychiatrist.

Let the child vent that anger, but make sure it's aimed in the right direction—at the person who killed himself. It is natural and healthy to feel angry at being abandoned by a loved one who has committed suicide. Psychiatrist Bruce Danto suggests that one way to help direct that anger is by letting older children read the suicide note, if there is one. Then they'll know the facts. If they don't, they may make them up. With honest information about what happened, the suicide can be handled in a straightforward, factual manner. That will help keep the youngster in touch with reality, and show the desperation or confusion of the person who died. "Look, you have a right to read this and be angry. Being angry at someone you love doesn't mean that you don't love them." Reassure the child that you will not abandon him in this way: "Don't worry; I would never do that to you. I would never kill myself. I'm really angry at him because he dumped on us. He was a desperate man, he couldn't see any other way out."

Danto stresses the importance of telling the child that the person who committed suicide chose the *wrong way* to solve his problems. Other people have problems and they don't kill themselves. Don't glorify the dead person—make a therapeutic split between him and the survivors. "It takes more courage to live. That he opted for a different way is his problem." By talking in this way, Danto says you help the child mobilize his anger against the dead person, getting the grieving process started.

Besides guilt and anger, children will also probably have to cope with the stigma associated with suicide. Many of us have been told since childhood that people who commit suicide go to hell. Others figure the person was crazy and that the rest of the family must be too. The family members who are left are traumatized, their stability shaken.

When someone in the family commits suicide, a child gets several different messages. One concerns his or her own worth. "I am not lovable enough for him to have hung around for." A second perceived message may be that he or she is a loser, says Bruce Danto. "The child may feel he is being told, 'Look kid, I couldn't make it and neither can you.' " Danto notes that when you break the news to a child that a person he loved has committed suicide, you have to change these perceived messages around so that the child can regain a sense of his own self-worth.

In an article published in *The New York Times*, journalist Lisa Bergson, whose mother committed suicide when she was seven, talked about how her brother felt as he tried to resume life in the house they had shared with their mother. "I was no longer a normal kid," he said. "It's like you're a bit of a freak because of what's happened in your family."

Sometimes there are cases where, for one reason or another, a suicide is not labeled as such. Families who are certain that the death was a suicide and who choose to conceal this from their children should be aware of the risks involved. David Peretz, a psychiatrist at Columbia University in New York, points out a couple of these risks. The children may overhear conversations, get a sense that they are not being told the whole story, and then create their own fantasies about what happened. Also, they may find out years later that they have been lied to about this matter of great importance, and then wonder what other lies they've been told. Dr. Peretz says, "It's hard enough to deal with a child when we *know* what he thinks, but when we don't know what he thinks it's almost impossible."

Whether the suicide was intentional or sub-intentional— whether the person was aware at the time that he was actually killing himself—it is vitally important that parents convince their children how wrong it was. As we know, a child often models his behavior after that of his parents and others around him, and the evidence is clear that this "modeling" is particularly strong in cases of suicide. I have personally dealt with five cases that were almost the exact duplicates of the suicides of relatives. In one instance, not only were the same site and method used, but it took place at the same hour and on the same day.

A man I know whose father had jumped off a building five years before came in to make arrangements for his brother, who had just done the same thing. Tortured and devastated, he asked me, "Is this the way my family's supposed to die?" This "follow the leader" syndrome is sometimes rooted in romanticism, sometimes in certain feelings of destiny. Whatever the root, it's a connection that must be broken, with discussion, love, and in many cases, therapy.

Suicides of Children

When a young child thinks of killing himself, he often thinks that suicide is just a temporary thing. Not aware of the finality of death, he sees it as an immediate solution to his problems, or an ultimate punishment for his parents. With the pre-adolescent, suicide may be triggered when the child is abused, depressed, or rejected. Magical thinking takes over, and he may believe that he will be rescued later, like Snow White was. When a teenager commits suicide, however, the reasons are usually much more complicated.

According to Jane Brody, writing in *The New York Times*, the suicide rate among young people under nineteen years of age has increased by about 300 percent since the 1950s. Each day, an average of eighteen adolescents kill themselves. Besides the reasons I've already described for suicide, young people have the added burdens of growing up in a transient society, in which upwardly mobile parents often don't take the time to talk with their children about their problems. Widespread use of drugs and alcohol often alter youngsters' senses of reality and help push them on the way to self-destruction. The rash of teenage suicides in the Dallas suburb of Plano and in New York's Westchester County in the past few years prompted many of people to take a closer look at the problem and try to do something about it. As I mentioned earlier, courses on death and dying have been set up in a number of high schools and colleges around the country. Openness in talking about suicide removes some of the magic and mystery that teenagers find so appealing; it also helps break the impulse to "follow the leader."

Try to handle suicide as conventionally as possible, mourning it as you would any other death, with a funeral and open grieving for the dead person. This will take some of the horror and stigma away. If you allow a child to go to the funeral home, to talk about the dead person, and look at him and touch him if he wants to, he'll be better able to confront the death and start to grieve. As with other deaths, putting a note in the casket or bringing a goodbye present may help him to "make amends," to say goodbye. The child will probably be feeling a lack of security, so he should be told as soon as possible that he will be taken care of, who will be taking care of him, and that he's going to be safe and loved.

Trying to pretend that the person never existed, or that the harm done to the family is so devastating that the person should never be talked about again, will only hurt the survivors more, especially the children. They need to know that trust exists in the family, no matter what trauma they've been through; as always, talking about the problem and the feelings everyone is experiencing will help them to better cope with the crisis.

3.

Grief and Healing

Seventeen-year-old Amy sat in the parlor car of the train, looking out the window and going over every minute of the last few days in her mind. Her sister and mother sat across from her, absorbed in their books. But Amy could do nothing but stare out the window and listen to the beat of the train against the tracks. Her mind was frozen with anxiety.

Back in Memphis, in a grave not yet marked with a stone, lay her grandmother. She had been quite a lady—a poet, a gardener, a gentlewoman—and to Amy, a kind and sensitive best friend to talk to. Only six people had shown up at the funeral, and as the young priest stood on the altar behind the casket, he intoned words that would stick in Amy's mind for a lifetime. "Everyone is precious in God's eyes—the great and famous, and the little people like Margaret here, who go about their lives quietly, never making much of an impression, never seeming to make much of a difference. . . ." The words went around and around in Amy's head as she tried to make some sense out of it all; all the while rage was growing inside her. Her grandmother was important, she *did* make a difference. The world was a better place because of her!

In Amy's family, people didn't talk about their feelings. That kind of thing was dismissed as sentimental and self-indulgent. Actions were more important than words. If something bothered you, you worked it out yourself. So, Amy's pain and resentment smoldered inside her for months. She never cried. A couple of years later it all burst forth in a severe depression. Fortunately, she had a boyfriend who was sensitive and a good listener; he helped her to heal.

Teenagers, young children, adults . . . everyone needs a release valve, someone to be the catalyst to help them work their feelings out. Without this catalyst, a wall is built up around the grieving person. Sometimes, as in Amy's case, we do much of the construction ourselves. Amy's mother didn't even know the wall was there. But very often, especially in the case of small children, the parents do the handiwork, creating a sturdy barrier that they think will protect their child from pain.

This wall tends to be made of fairy tales, incomplete messages, suppressed emotions. Does it do the job parents expect it to? Maybe, in the case of infants, it does. But professionals agree that once a child is over the age of two or three, it isn't an effective strategy. Step on the other side of the wall and take a look at your child. Do you see a youngster who's relatively happy or one who's really upset? It could be that he or she is confused, or grieving, and not getting enough support. That's a problem that can certainly be remedied, now that you are equipped with the right tools.

In this chapter we will look at the ways in which children cope with death and grief, and see how you can help the healing process. Again, let me remind you that you might not find the exact answer to your situation outlined here, because each situation is unique. I hope you will take what applies to you and work it into your family blueprint.

Sometimes parents come in and ask me to talk to their children myself, to explain death to them, and I always tell the parents the same thing. "You are the ones who are with the children day to day, and it is you they will come to three months down the road with questions." There is a little saying that applies here: If you give a man a fish, you feed him for a day; but if you give him a hook and teach him to fish, you feed him for a lifetime. Certainly, it would be easier if I or some other outside person did the talking, but it would be only a temporary relief. Who will answer the questions at three o'clock in the morning when the child wakes up wondering where Grandpa is? It's difficult watching your child grieve, but once you've broken down the wall and opened the channels of communication with your child, you'll know what to expect, how he'll react, and how to help him.

Start by asking yourself a few questions. First, how close was your child to the person who died? If it was just a casual acquaintance, a neighbor down the street of whom he was only vaguely aware, the child will probably not be too upset. But if it was a family member or classmate, someone who was really a part of his life, the child may be devastated—not only by the death, but by the fact that the routine of his life will be in an upheaval. Things will not be going the way they usually do, and that can be very unsettling for a child.

A second thing to consider is what kind of person the child is. Children, like adults, have different personalities, so they grieve differently when they're in a crisis. Some are stoic, others get hysterical; some withdraw, others throw themselves into activities; some are philosophical and accepting, others are angry and belligerent. The differences in reaction are due in part to the way the child has been taught to behave. In each family there are certain patterns of behavior that are acceptable. The members of one family may be demonstrative, warm, and affectionate with each other. In another family, they'll be more reserved.

The child's family background helps give him stability and a framework in which to work out his grief. Most bereavement counselors I've talked to agree, however, that children from demonstrative families have an easier time getting through grief because they've already learned how to show their emotions.

COMMON REACTIONS TO GRIEF

How do children faced with a death express their grief? Here are some kinds of behavior that you might expect to see.

Exhaustion

Many children who are experiencing grief for the first time will have physical symptoms like exhaustion. Sixteen-year-old Anne felt as though someone had pulled a plug and drained all her energy out of her. "I can hardly walk up the stairs," she sighed. While she focused her effort on trying to get over her grief, there was less energy left for other things.

Other common reactions are sleeping much of the time ("I just want to make the world go away"); loss of appetite ("I can't eat. The food tastes like sandpaper"); and lethargy ("She just sits there like a bump on a log, doing nothing").

Dependency

"She won't do anything unless someone else suggests it and actually goes along with her. She can't seem to make decisions. And she used to be so independent!" This need for support in the extreme, where the child becomes very dependent, attaching him or herself to others, is part of the state of disorganization that often accompanies grief. Not able to initiate and maintain their own activities, helpless and afraid of being alone, the children are in a sense reaching out to those around them.

Feelings of Unreality

In the early days after a death, a number of youngsters have said that they felt as though this were happening to someone else, that they were watching a movie with themselves in it. "Someone who looks like me is standing here. And those people look like my family. But it just can't be!" Feeling empty, alone, and out of control, the child wants to be with the person who died . . . to touch him and sit and talk with him.

One child explained: "It's as though part of *me* has died." The child is still able to function, even go to school or talk with friends, but there is a feeling that he is going about the routine of his life without thinking, filled with a sense of unreality.

Panic

Afraid that some other devastating thing is going to happen, afraid of being alone at night, afraid of he doesn't even know what, a child may feel a sense of panic as he tries to put the death of the person in perspective and go on with his life. Depressed, vulnerable, tired, and listless, the feelings overwhelm him. "I just don't know what to do," seven-year-old Brendan sobbed. "Nobody can help me, I feel so bad." Fortunately, that little boy had a mother and a sister who sat beside him every night for two weeks while he went through his night terrors. When a child has this sense of panic, this anxiety, he needs to be told that it will pass, that in time he'll be okay and that he'll be able to think about the person who died and not have the pain. He needs to be given hope.

Preoccupation With the Dead Person

Preoccupation with the person who died is another very common symptom of grief. Everything reminds the child of that person, and in trying to distance himself from his pain, the child may pull away from his friends and family.

A few weeks after the death of her father, fourteen-year-old Linda just couldn't stop thinking about him. Over and over again, she played the scenes of their times together in her mind. Whenever anyone tried to divert her, she became irritable. She also had difficulty sleeping, and sometimes at two o'clock in the morning you could find her in her room, trying to read herself to sleep. "Sometimes I felt so weird I thought I was going crazy," she remembered. "All I could think about was my daddy and how he was dead."

To identify with the dead person, a child even occasionally starts imitating his actions, walking as he walked, doing things that he might have done. Joseph, a twelve-year-old, became the family handyman after his father died, slipping into the role of Mr. Fix-it just like his father. When a friend came over to help fix the boiler, Joseph went down the basement with him, all the while giving advice: "This is how

my father would do it." Sliding into that role was good for
Joseph; he had found his niche. It gave him a little sense of
control and helped him find an anchor during the mourning
period. Sometimes, though, this imitation and identification
can be negative. Meg's grandmother was chronically sick
during her whole life. Right after she died, thirteen-year-old
Meg, who was very close to her, developed chronic migraine
headaches, just like her grandmother. She needed professional help before she got over them.

Hyperactivity

Some children, as they're mourning, become hyperactive,
hopping from thing to thing aimlessly, searching for something to do. In their restlessness they act as though they've
been plugged into an electrical socket, and you may look
with wonder at them. "Where do they get that energy?"
Some children talk incessantly, others laugh when they feel
like crying; but no amount of talking or laughing seems to
ease their minds.

Destructive Behavior

One mild-mannered young fellow all of a sudden became
hostile and obnoxious when an aunt he adored died. Feeling
helpless and full of despair, he lashed out at those around
him, completely out of character. When his mother helped
him talk his feelings out, he calmed down again. Another
child, a ten-year-old who was unable to express his grief after
his father died, tried to bring those feelings out in a physical
way. Sitting under a table at the memorial service, the boy
tugged at the tablecloth, bringing the memorial candle that
was sitting on top of the table closer and closer to the edge.
This kind of destructive misbehavior is not a common reac-

tion; it's highly unusual, but it points up what can happen in the mind of a child who doesn't know how to talk about what's bothering him. If your child experiences a big behavior change, and it lasts more than a few days, you may need extra help to guide him through his grief.

Regression

Regression is a common symptom of grief. Six-year-olds who have been toilet trained for years may suddenly revert to wetting the bed. Preteens, usually very much in touch with reality, may slide back into the magical thinking of a preschooler. In one dramatic case, a ten-year-old whose grandmother had died opened the window of his apartment, planning to jump out. Later, when he was asked which way he'd go if he took the leap, the boy said, "Up." Desperately lonely for his grandmother, who had raised him, he regressed into magical thinking and reasoned that by jumping out the window, he'd be reunited with his grandmother, who he believed was up in the clouds, in heaven.

That, of course, is an extreme example, and that child obviously needed extra help to get over his reunification fantasy, his magical thinking, and his pain. But it's clear that children can be severely affected by the death of those close to them. Years ago, it was thought that children were incapable of grief. How wrong that thinking is!

If a child's life is already in turmoil, if he or she is having trouble at home or at school, there will probably be more trouble dealing with the death than if life had been relatively calm. An adult, feeling shaky and vulnerable in an unsteady job, might feel as though the rug has been pulled from under him when someone close to him dies. A teenager who feels that his parents or his friends don't understand him may look on a death in the family as just another disaster that he has to face. Overwhelmed and particularly vulnerable, this child will need extra support.

THE SPECIAL NEEDS OF CHILDREN

Even when children seem to be handling a death well—"just like an adult," as people often put it—they may be confused, filled with fears they find it difficult to express. They need that extra bit of support, attention, and understanding that we don't tend to give to other adults.

I remember one poignant scene. A twelve-year-old boy whose father had died stood by the casket with his mother, greeting the guests. Dressed in a suit and tie, he looked responsible, stable, the man of the family now. His body language said it all, however: stooped over, as though he were carrying the weight of the world on his shoulders; a blank expression, as though someone had turned out the light inside him; a face filled with pain. Life had dealt him a really rotten blow and he was handling it, but inside that façade was a little boy who was desperately afraid. He had not yet been able to start his grieving process.

Take a look at your child's face. Are the muscles tight? Does he seem to be in a state of tension, hostile and hard to talk to? Then maybe he's running away from the issue. On the other hand, it could be that he doesn't really understand the finality of death, which, as I've pointed out, is often the case with a young child. "What's the big deal? Why is everyone so upset?" he or she might think. "Grandpa will only be dead for a little while." An adult who is mourning someone dear to the family can find it unnerving when he thinks that his child doesn't really care that the person died. What he has to realize, when the child is crying bitterly one moment then laughing and jumping around the next, is that the child has also been mourning Grandpa, but he can only handle so much grief. He needs to switch to a different activity at a certain point. We adults often have to do this too, when we're confronted with too much pain—we watch TV, go on a walk, talk on the telephone.

Peter, a teenager I know, played in a tennis match the morning after his father died. In another family, the mother might have found that hard to take. But Peter's mother knew what to expect. She had already sat down with Peter and together they had decided that although Peter was very sad, he would go ahead with the match, that his father would probably have wanted him to play. Peter's mother realized that she couldn't expect a child to grieve as an adult would.

Sometimes in a crisis we adults confuse our own reactions to a death with our child's, projecting on the young person what we're feeling ourselves. John's father had just died and he was deeply disturbed, angry, and feeling guilty because he hadn't spent more time with him. He was generally just miserable. One day it came to a head. "Why are you always so depressed?", he lashed out at his teenage daughter. "Moping around, in a lousy mood. Try to cheer up!" The astonished girl hadn't been feeling blue at all. She wasn't the one who was upset; her father was, and since he couldn't admit his feelings to himself, he projected them onto her. A person who isn't able to come to grips with his own feelings can cause double trouble in the family, putting everyone more on edge than they had been when the death first occurred. Children can do this as well as adults. Being aware of this possibility and talking about it can help prevent a lot of pain.

Very often a child may not seem to be a bit upset about the death of a person he was very close to; he may act as though nothing has happened. It could be that he is avoiding the issue. Maybe he's been getting mixed messages from his parents and feels confused; or maybe he's not ready to deal with it, just as we adults sometimes steer away from unpleasant things we want to avoid.

Four-year-old Sandy was very confused. His mother was crying all the time and when he asked why, she said she had a stomachache. Later, after we had talked about the problem, the mother told Sandy that it was because Grandpa had died and that she was very, very sad because she wouldn't be seeing Grandpa again. Sandy replied, "Don't tell me that story anymore."

That was not an uncommon reply for a child to make. Sandy had had enough. He was confused for the moment, and children tend to shut out things they can't handle. A week or so later, Sandy came back with his questions—he was able to deal with his feelings by then.

Perhaps your child's reaction is concern and regret about the death, but not upset. Some people, children included, are just not that emotional.

Sean, age fifteen, is a very mature, philosophical kind of young man who has always been thought to be much older than his years. While many of his friends experience great highs and lows, Sean goes through life on an even keel. "When my grandfather died," he explained, "sure, I was sad. For a moment I felt a little rattled, but then I went into a different mode. I felt that that's the way things are—people have to die someday. I didn't feel guilty or angry; he knew how much I cared for him. And as things in the family became crazier, I got calmer and cooler. The way I looked at it was that my function was to help the rest of the family. There was no question of my feeling like breaking down. I haven't felt like crying in years. That's just not my way of expressing it." Sean added that if it had been his father who died, he might have reacted differently. "My life wasn't as intimately intertwined with Grandpa's as it is with my dad's."

Sean had found his own style of grieving. It was not highly emotional, but neither was it an avoidance of the problem. He talked quietly about his grandfather and told stories about things they had done together, remembering him fondly. Sean didn't need a lot of help to handle the crisis of death, but many youngsters his age do need that extra help.

THE GRIEVING PROCESS

Each person needs to discover his or her own way of grieving. Trying to stop one child's process by saying something like "Be brave, be a man!" minimizes the loss and puts an unbelievable burden on that child. To work out their feelings, most children need someone to talk to. Just as the warmth of the sun heals the body, sharing what he feels with someone who cares helps the child heal. For many, tears are therapeutic—a tribute of love for someone who was very dear to them. Others, as I've pointed out, may never shed any tears. If we don't put demands or limitations on our children, by trying to change their grieving process or pretending that it's not going on, the child will grow with the experience.

If you try to cut short the child's grieving process, it may just cause a delayed reaction. In one study on grieving, a story was told about a teenager who had lost both her parents and her boyfriend in a fire. She was left to take care of her younger brothers and sisters. At first she showed cheerful acceptance, then after about two months the impact of the deaths finally hit her. Her responsibilities and the need to maintain the morale of her brothers and sisters had delayed her grieving process. In another really bizarre case, an obviously successful, well-dressed man came to my funeral home once a year on the anniversary of the death of his father, looking for him. Finally, a couple of years ago, he stopped coming, having resolved his grief in some way.

The sudden realization—the breaking of dammed-up feelings—can come at any time, and be triggered by the most innocuous things. Twelve-year-old Bridget was walking down the aisle of the grocery store when all of a sudden tears started streaming down her face. She had seen a box of Instant Ralston, her father's favorite kind of cereal, and it had triggerd the release valve for her feelings.

When something like that happens, the time to deal with what that child is feeling is right then—as soon as possible. Don't put it off until a later, more convenient time. Bridget's mother for example, put her arms around her daughter and let her cry for a minute or two; then the child felt better and they went on with their shopping.

Three Stages of Grief

Dr. John Bowlby of the Tavistock Clinic in London, working with bereaved children, has observed that there are three stages of grief that most children go through—protest, pain, and, finally, hope.

In the protest stage, the youngster can't believe that the person is dead and tries to get him or her back. One five-year-old I know enlisted the help of a playmate and went to work in her backyard one afternoon, digging up about $300 worth of sod. "I'm looking for Grandpa," she explained to her mother, who came upon the scene about an hour too late. "I miss him. I want him to come home." The little girl, who had been told that Grandpa had died and was buried (although she didn't know anything about where he was buried), figured she'd undo the deed.

The child who faces the death of someone he's loved needs to turn his energies into himself, to talk about how he misses that person. By bringing all the memories to the conscious surface, bit by bit, the child will gradually come to terms with the loss, realizing that the person is dead but never forgotten. The child may need to talk a lot about the dead person, describing in detail all his qualities, how tragic it is that his life was cut short, and how important he was to the youngster. With time, he'll be able to put the memory of the deceased into perspective and move on.

"If you want to heal folks, learn to lay ears on them," writes Doug Manning of Hereford, Texas, in his book *A Minister Speaks About Funerals.* Manning says that by just sitting there listening and not saying much, we can do a tremendous amount of good. He reminds us that people have to solve their own problems; we can't work out someone else's thinking or his feelings. What we can do is stimulate a person to work them out for himself while he talks out what's on his mind. But, cautions Manning, listening is hard to do. "We feel we must say something. To not have an answer is to somehow prove we are not competent. . . . One of the startling discoveries of my life was when I noticed how trained I was to talk and how untrained I was to listen."

The trouble with memories, as Dennis Klass and Audrey Gordon point out in *They Need to Know,* is that before we share them, before we get the feelings out, we act and feel as if the events were in the present when they are actually in the past. By sharing the memories and resolving the feelings, "the present can get some control over the past," and reality takes the place of fantasy.

Kathy had an abusive father. For years she had hoped he'd die or that her parents would get a divorce; anything to get her father out of her life. One night he got drunk, was hit by a car, and died. "I'm glad he's dead," she admitted sometime later. "I had wished he would die for a long time and now I'm relieved. That's a terrible way to feel. . . . I know I didn't cause him to die but I still feel guilty that I wished so hard."

Once a feeling is expressed, no matter how negative, it doesn't have the power that it did when it was formless. When feelings are put on the table, talked out and looked at in a realistic perspective, they often lose their impact.

As we listen to our children, remember that it's important to make sure that we hear what they're actually saying, not what we *think* they should be saying. We might expect our child to feel lonely or sad, but what comes out of him is that he's relieved or feeling guilty that the person died. His feelings may be very different from what we ourselves are feeling. The temptation is to try and change him. "You shouldn't feel guilty. You did everything you could to help him stay alive"; or, "Even though he treated you badly, he was your father, so you shouldn't feel relieved that he died."

Telling a child he shouldn't feel a certain way, judging his feelings, is an automatic turn-off. Don't judge him, just listen. He has a right to his feelings. They're part of him and he needs to work them out. What he needs to know is that he is not alone; that you're there to help him; that you accept the way he is, bad feelings and all; and that you're trying to empathize. Maybe you've felt that way, too—if so, you can understand what's happening inside him right now. Reassure him that it's okay, it's normal to have these emotions, and that eventually the pain will pass.

The second stage of grief that Dr. John Bowlby described is a time of pain, despair, and disorganization. By this time the child realizes that the person is gone forever, and as reality sets in, he may be overwhelmed with feelings of anger and guilt, loneliness, and depression. I'll talk more about these feelings in the pages ahead.

Finally, during the third stage of grief, the child realizes that no matter how much he loved the person, he can continue life without him, and he begins to reorganize his life. He begins to find the feeling of hope.

It is during this time—after the pain has eased up, when the good days outnumber the bad—that the child will get involved again in things and see options for the future. It may happen at a very definite moment. In one case, the moment of letting go came when a girl helped her mother clean out her father's desk; another child gave away his father's fishing rod in a symbolic gesture of goodbye. But it takes time before a child can make that independent move.

It's important to remember that all of the feellings associated with grief ebb and flow, and that you and your child will inevitably go back over these emotions time and again. We love to neatly compartmentalize things, to finish with one, then go on to the next. But it doesn't work that way with the emotions of grief.

Like Sean, the fifteen-year-old I talked about earlier, your child might not go through many of the emotions. Gwen Schwartz-Borden, a social worker who does bereavement counseling on Long Island, New York, remembered one woman who came to her after reading a book on dealing with grief. Very upset, she asked, "Am I going to go crazy like this book says? I've never been a person who acted crazy!" The woman thought that there must be some recipe for grief, and because she didn't feel crazy she wasn't following directions; she wasn't doing it right!

How long does the grieving process take? According to the late Dr. Erich Lindeman, that depends on how well the person does the "grief work." During this process, a person frees himself from his bond to the dead person, readjusts his life, and forms new relationships. It may go more quickly for some than for others. Dr. Hal Fishkin compares the process to a sore that needs to heal. "If you have a wound, you clean it and expose it to fresh air and the light of day. Then you take away all the damaged tissue and make it as clean as possible so that normal healing can take place . . . and that takes time." He adds that after six months the child who has lost someone very close to him probably won't be as depressed as he was after two weeks, but that it's difficult to generalize. "Different children need different things. Some have such a turbulent emotional response that they need much more help."

Some people who aren't able to work out their grief never resolve it; they may learn to live with their pain, but it never leaves. Most youngsters are able to bounce back with resiliency; remember, though, that grief is an emotion that recurs sporadically. Almost anything can trigger the pain—a song, the smell of a certain flower; an anniversary or holiday, even as much as a year later, can be the worst time. Gwen Schwartz-Borden notes that just when you think you're better, the pain can start up again. "Just when reality sets in and the numbness wears off, months after the death, it may all of a sudden hit the child again . . . all that yearning and searching for the dead person. It's like a woman with false labor pains."

PROBLEMS TO BE PREPARED FOR
AT VARIOUS AGES

Much of what we've covered so far in this chapter has been how older children react to a death. They're the ones who usually have a tougher time and take longer to work through their pain and anxiety. With little children, we have to spend more time finding out what they think, clearing up misconceptions, and helping them understand that the person is really dead forever. Young children also experience pain—it may not last as long as that of an older child, but it is still often very severe.

In Chapter 1, we took a look at what children in each major age group might think and understand about death. The children in each of these groups also have predictable reactions when confronted with the death of someone close to them.

Age Two to Six

Little children will probably be clingy, afraid to let you go out, concerned that they'll lose you, too. Over and over again they might ask, "Hasn't he been dead enough?" Don't get frustrated. Death is a hard concept for little ones to understand, and eventually it'll sink in. With fewer resources to help them deal with their feelings, they still have to go through the same stages of grief that an adult or older child does. To make things more complicated, their minds are also filled with magical thinking. According to Gwen Schwartz-Borden, that magical thinking and the "I did it" syndrome are the most common problems bereaved children have— waiting for the dead person to come back, or thinking that they caused the death of the person.

The very young child usually doesn't know that he's grieving, he just knows that he feels bad—and since he usually doesn't have the vocabulary or the experience to explain what he's feeling, he speaks to us in symbolic language, acting out his feelings in fantasy play.

> Bill, John, and Mary Ellen were very close to Grandpa. He lived on the next block in the city, just a two-minute bicycle ride around the corner, and each summer they all went to the country together. During the first summer after Grandpa died the children seldom talked about him, but he was still a part

of their lives. They played in the backyard, watching the chipmunk (which Grandpa had confided told him secrets!), and pulling the weeds out of the garden that the old man had tended so carefully. Finally one afternoon they locked themselves in their room, and, taking all the clothes out of the dresser drawer, they lined it with a blanket. Next, they put candles on top of the bureau and opened a prayer book to prayers for the dead. Bill and John then dressed up in sheets so they'd look like priests and they put Mary Ellen in the dresser drawer, their make-believe coffin. She lay there quietly while Bill and John sang their funeral songs. All three children participated in their make-believe funeral, saying goodbye to Grandpa. Years later, the three of them still talk about that afternoon with fondness. Theirs was a family where the children felt free to grieve in the way they chose.

Remember that when we try to explain something, we use our minds to form the ideas into words, very often pushing away the feelings. Since children don't have the command of the language that we do or the experience to express how they feel, they often relate nonverbally, on an emotional level, understanding a look in your eyes or the gentle tone of your voice just as much as the words you're saying. Allow your child to be open and express how he feels. Then he'll be comfortable enough to come back for more information. Children adjust more quickly when they feel that they're in on things, and that their parents understand how they're feeling. By talking with your child in an open, direct manner, by holding his hand and letting him cry, you say, "I understand, I'm with you."

Sharing your feelings with a young child on a level he'll understand can help him realize that his own feelings are okay. Here's what you might say to a three- or four-year-old: "I feel very, very sad that Grandpa died, and very, very mad because Grandpa didn't take good care of himself and he didn't take his medicine like he was supposed to. I wanted him to live. We'll all be lonesome for Grandpa and we'll miss him a lot and sometimes we'll be crying." More information can be added, depending on the age and maturity of the child.

One researcher in the field of child bereavement described the way a little boy whose brother had died handled his grief in his fantasy play: he buried his brother's toys in the sandbox. Gradually, the child worked through his grief: his parents put a picture of the dead child in the boy's room; the family started to talk about how they missed his brother; and finally, one by one, the child removed the toys from the sandbox and put them back on the shelf.

Jenny's mother was similarly sensitive to her child's reactions. After her mother had explained the facts, four-year-old Jenny asked when she could see Grandpa again. Her mother explained, "Not for a long, long time, after you die and get buried and go to heaven." But Jenny, like many children her age, was persistent. "Will God make him better and send him back?" "No," answered the mother. "Once a person's body stops working, it won't work anymore, and he is dead. He won't come back." The mother said Jenny accepted that pretty well, after she had cried for a while. "Then I said, 'No matter what happens, you still have me.' And she's seemed fine ever since."

Age Six to Nine

Very often, children in this age group may be preoccupied with morbid thoughts, fascinated by the image of death stalking around, scared of the bogey man. Louise was that age, in the early days of grammar school, when the reclusive old lady next door to her died. The word got around that the old lady's house was haunted, and that her ghost snatched children who walked by at night. The street was off limits for months, with the children in the neighborhood taking great precautions to avoid that block on their way to school. Louise, by association, was singled out. After all, she had been the lady's next-door neighbor, and she was a rather shy girl, so she was labeled weird and creepy; she didn't have one friend; the children avoided her. Not able to understand why they feel afraid or confused, children at this age sometimes try to find a scapegoat to embody their fears.

If they're embarrassed or don't know how to behave, they may act silly or laugh; on the other hand, they may become suddenly quiet when they see a person who in their mind is associated with death. Stevie, a nine-year-old whose father had just died, noticed that the other kids wouldn't "goof off" if he was around. Maybe they felt that when someone dies everyone should always act serious. But for Stevie, so recently traumatized by his father's death, the reaction of his classmates made this time even harder. Suddenly, he was not only alone in his grief, he was an outsider. Children need to be told what to say and how to act when someone dies. Most of them are probably not aware of how they may be hurting other children.

At this age, children coping with a death may be feeling guilty or angry, or may be afraid that their parents will die. They often show their concern with questions such as, "How old are you?" (meaning, "Are you going to die too?"), or with increased interest in a parent's health. Explaining away his fears will help him feel better:

> "Remember how cranky Grandpa was the last few times we saw him? Well, that's because he was so sick. Some children might think that they did something that caused a person to die—that maybe because they talked back to him or made too much noise and got him upset, that's why he died. But those things just don't make people die."

As with the younger children, playing often helps older ones to work out their stressful situations. It is through play, say the experts, that a child can achieve mastery over a situation he doesn't understand and work through his anxiety. Some children paint sad pictures; others might play violent games in which cars crash and burn to get their feelings out. Encourage your child to talk about the dead person, to relive the good times and the bad. Unlike the younger child, who probably remembers just the surface aspects (what he looked like, the fact that he had curly hair), the "middle" child remembers more enduring qualities—the fact that Grandma used to go on walks with her and tell her stories; the fact that she was kind and funny. And it's those qualities this child will probably miss. "He won't be sitting at his favorite place in the bleachers watching me play ball anymore." "Who will go blueberry-picking with me now?"

When there's a death close to home, the world may seem to be tumbling down. Eight-year-old Kevin's mother died. Right at the same time a tropical plant that the family had brought back from a vacation, nurturing it and growing from a seedling, wilted and died. Then, on the day of the funeral, Kevin and his father walked into their house and found their pet bird lying dead in its cage. The child was very upset. "What is it about us that makes everything die?" Kevin's father had to help him understand that these events were completely unrelated ("We were visiting Mom at the hospital so much I forgot to water the plants," etc.).

Age Nine to Twelve

Trying to be grownup, the preteen is still at least some of the time in the world of fantasy. He or she probably grasps death intellectually but may be having a hard time letting it sink in. Children this age do not want to seem different from the other kids. "How should I act?" "What do I say to Grandma?" They can also be very judgmental about themselves and everyone around them. "I really looked so stupid crying. I shouldn't have been so upset. I knew she was sick. . . ." "Aunt Molly really put on a scene. Was I embarrassed!" "Grandpa looked really gross! Lying there in the casket he looked really phoney!"

Becoming very much their own people, children this age may be critical or sensitive, catty or kind. Bridget, the pre-teen we met earlier in the aisles of the supermarket, used to come into her mother's room and sit quietly holding her hand when she knew her mother was crying . . . not saying a word, just being there to let her mother know she cared. Bryan, another sensitive child, feeling irritable and confused, didn't want to bother other people with his grief—so he isolated himself in his room every night, afraid he might antagonize his friends. Each thing that he tried seemed to take an enormous amount of effort and it made him frustrated, short-tempered. After a month or so he had worked things through, and he started coming out of his room and getting involved in things again. "Boy, I guess I never realized how important Grandpa was to me," he finally said.

Teenagers

By the time a child is in his teens, he will probably have many of the same feelings and reactions to a death that an adult would. But the way he processes his grief—his behavior— may be very different. A wildly hysterical outburst may be followed immediately by embarrassed laughter as the child tries to get a grip on himself, to act like an adult. One moment he may idealize the dead person, making him super-human, the next moment condemn him. His emotions may be in an uproar and he doesn't know how to help himself.

Teenagers are very concerned with their image and what the other kids think of them, and sometimes when they are actually raging against the world they appear to be strong, stoic, and cool. They often hate having people see them cry. Because of this, their emotions may erupt in physical distress—changes in the nervous or hormonal system, headaches, hyperventilation or hyperactivity. A girl's menstrual period may stop for a few months. Another child may act indifferent, expressing helplessness by pretending the death didn't happen. Still another may criticize what's happening around him, or philosophize about how futile life is. In the crisis of death, a teenager's whole system of belief may be thrown topsy-turvy, and a child who's disturbed may start acting very much out of character; in extreme situations, trying to forget through overeating, alcohol, or drugs. Very often at the base of that compulsive behavior are two of the common elements of grief: anger and guilt.

DEALING WITH ANGER, GUILT, AND RESPONSIBILITY

The backyard looked like a monsoon had struck it—swamped with water, some of the puddles two inches deep. It was a day to sit inside and read a book or watch television, but eleven-year-old Ted wanted to go camping. He had taken his tent out of his closet and was starting to ready all his gear when his father happened to walk by his room. "What are you up to?" the father asked. "I'm going to pitch my tent in the backyard," Ted answered. "You can't do that! It's pouring out there!" "I'm going to do it anyhow," Ted said angrily.

Several days before, Ted's uncle had died and the emotions had been building steadily inside him. He was ready to burst. He didn't know what to do, but he had to do something, so he decided to put up his tent. When his father questioned this, he lashed out; fortunately, his father understood what was happening, and after they sat down together and talked it all out, the gear went back in the closet.

People get angry because, like Ted, they feel out of control, impotent, helpless. Anger is an emotion that's hard to express openly, because showing it is generally not acceptable in our society. If you don't express it in some way, though, it's hard to shake. It may burst out in all sorts of ways—shouting at friends, snide remarks to a teacher, a hostile reaction when a parent asks a question.

When a person dies, there are plenty of things to be angry about. Your child might be angry at the doctor for not being able to cure the person, at God for not making him better, at you for not making the person who died take his medicine, even at the person who died for self-destructive behavior or abandoning the family. This anger may be justified. You can imagine the rage a child would feel at the drunken driver who killed his mother! In other circumstances, the anger may be misplaced.

One man told me that once he was just about to throw another guy through the window of a restaurant for a nasty remark when he suddenly stopped in mid-fight and realized what he was doing. "At the moment, I remembered that you had said I might be angry with my father for dying. At the time I thought to myself, 'Oh, I wouldn't do that.' Well, here I was, about ready to kill this guy, and I suddenly realized why I was so mad."

Anger is an emotion I see frequently as a funeral director. I see people frustrated at not being able to help the one that they loved survive, and so they lash out at those closest to them. Very often, kids pick up the anger of their parents, and what may look like arrogant, hostile misbehavior coming from youngsters may be suppressed anger. Each child will find his own way of ventilating that anger, satisfying the loss of control that he feels. Emily, a seven-year-old, chose the funeral home as the setting for bringing her anger to a head.

> Everyone in the family came to Grandpa's wake and Emily was even given a new dress for the occasion—a pretty light-blue smocked frock with lace. The family all went into the viewing room, gathering with the other relatives, talking and hugging each other. Even Emily's ten-year-old brother, George, was allowed in. But not Emily. She had to sit outside in the hall, and wait till the others came out. Looking back, Emily still remembers how angry she was to be left out like that. "I was so mad I wouldn't even talk about Grandpa. And I never wore that dress again. I absolutely refused. I wanted to let the family know how angry I was . . . that they should have let me come in with them. He was my grandpa and I wanted to say goodbye."

Occasionally, younger children may be more in touch with their feelings than older ones, whose minds have become muddled with all kinds of emotions. Bereavement counselor Gwen Schwartz-Borden tells the story of a five-year-old who told her that sometimes he gets really mad because his father died. And when he does, he beats up his brother. I'm glad I'm not that brother! But at least the mother knows what's happening when the boys get in a brawl. If the anger surfaces in the family, the moment may not be a pleasant one, but the parent gets a chance to see it firsthand and take steps to deal with it.

One way to deal with this anger is to encourage the child to express how angry he is, help him find some kind of outlet. Dan, a writer I know, told his daughter Maya that whenever he gets angry and frustrated, he goes out into the backyard with a tennis racket and beats the daylights out of a certain bush. Horticultural enthusiasts may not be very happy about this solution, but for this man it works. Maya decided her pillow was a better object of aggression and she spent a lot of time cleaning feathers out of her room. One father bought his son a punching bag to help him work out his anger at the loss of his younger brother; some people listen to music, others chop wood, go running, or scrub floors. Whatever releases the pent-up anger—as long as it doesn't hurt anyone—is fine.

But talking it all out is really the key to helping a child through the anger. If you feel angry too, you might say something like, "I'm really angry at Daddy for dying, and it makes me feel terrible that I feel that way because I know that he didn't want to die—but just the same, I do feel that way. And feelings are something that we can't control. We can control the way we act because of those feelings, but we can't control the feelings."

Anger is an emotion that is directed out at something; guilt is an emotion that is directed inward, often as a result of anger. The two go hand in hand when there's a death, and when they're allowed to fester they cause both adults and children a lot of grief.

"He shouldn't have gotten drunk that night." (Anger) "If only I had taken the keys away." (Guilt) "He shouldn't have run himself into the ground working so hard." (Anger) "If only I had realized what he was doing and tried to stop him, maybe he wouldn't have had the heart attack." (Guilt)

Children need the support of their parents or someone close to help them deal with these feelings and overcome the "I did it" syndrome. Caught in a vicious cycle of emotions, fifteen-year-old Kelly got angry at her father for dying, then felt guilty because of it, then angry again because she felt guilty. She felt she was losing her mind. Carol was just ten when her sister died after an illness of several months, during which her mother had to be at the hospital. "And all that time, I wished my sister would die because I wanted my mother back. When she did die, I felt relieved, but guilty, too." A couple of years later, her mother died. Emily, feeling that her wishful thinking had killed her sister, figured she was being punished with her mother's death. With no one to talk to about all this, she bottled up the feelings until she nearly burst.

Children, like adults, sometimes scourge themselves psychologically for not preventing the inevitable. "If only I hadn't put the stuffed animal in his crib last night" . . . "If only I hadn't gone to the store just at that moment." This guilt is irrational, as in the case of an eleven-year-old girl who blamed herself for never mailing a "get well" card to her aunt. "It was in my pocketbook, but I never took it to the mailbox," she kept repeating to her mother. The mother was amazed. "It's as though she thinks the card would have saved my sister's life."

Sometimes the guilt has a basis in fact. One teenaged girl was taking forever to brush her teeth, trying to push her father's patience to the limit. After about fifteen minutes, the father said to the child, "Come on now, you're making me sick!", and he clutched his chest. Within the hour, he was dead of a heart attack.

That unfortunate child did have something to do with her father's death and she required therapy to help work it through, but she wasn't the sole cause; she was just one of the final triggers. The man's heart was ready for an attack. The death had a biological cause.

Since guilt is often related to the cause of death, make sure your child has a good grasp of what happened to the dead person. Make him realize that there was something biologically wrong, so he won't be haunted for years by the thought that he could somehow have prevented it. When a child feels that there's no way to "make up" for a real or imagined wrong, when he has no chance to "do right" by the dead person, it's a terrific burden to carry.

One way to stop this kind of self-recrimination is to tell the children if you know that a person is very sick or dying. Give them a chance to say goodbye and say, "I'm sorry," to start working through whatever guilt they may have and deal with their grief. As Leo Lefebvre, a bereavement counselor in Delaware, points out, grief is a process we have to go through, and we grow according to how well we experience this process. There's no healthy way around it, only through it.

HELPING YOUR CHILD TO HEAL

Each person has his or her own mental metaphor for dealing with pain; sometimes it's religious, sometimes it's a physical technique. Gordon and Klass in *They Need to Know* describe one grieving technique for getting rid of unfinished business, those feelings of guilt, anger, and loss. They suggest that you and your child find a quiet place and sit down with a picture of the dead person; then, talking to the picture, get your child to express all the positive and negative feelings that are in his or her heart. "You may feel silly at first," they say, "but some people have found it helpful in saying goodbye."

Maybe there's a book or prayer that you turn to when you're upset, maybe a philosophical idea that makes you feel better when you think about it. Share these with your child. Dorothy told her grandchildren that when the world crashes in and she thinks she just can't handle things anymore, her trick is to "Golden Key the condition." In her mind, there's a big box that she puts troubles in . . . troubles that are beyond the grasp of everyday living. "And when things get to be too much, I just put the trouble in the box in my mind, lock it up with a golden key, and hand the key over to God."

As he passes through grief into healing, our youngster needs a continuity of care, one person to follow him through the experience—someone he trusts implicitly, someone he feels free to unload his feelings on. If you can't talk with your child (and some people just can't), find someone who can, a close friend or relative who will have the necessary patience and understanding and who will take the same approach that you're taking.

> Whenever there was a death in the family, Aunt Helen somehow always ended up with the little children. Children know when they can sit on someone's lap and when they can't; who they can confess to when they've been naughty, and who they had better steer clear of. And Aunt Helen was someone they could talk to.
> Death, in Aunt Helen's mind, wasn't anything to be feared. On warm spring afternoons she often took the little ones bike-riding down the paths of the neighborhood cemetery, pointing out the pretty flowers and where all the relatives were buried. Calm and accepting, Aunt Helen thought of death as a part of life. So, every time there was a wake in the family, Aunt Helen was the one who took care of the kids. She never got ruffled; the children felt comfortable with her and she with them.

As I've noted, how children react and how they heal are often affected by how the adults around them react. Sometimes a bereaved child who comes from a calm environment and is not used to seeing emotion overtly displayed can be threatened by open affection. Having relatives he hardly knows hugging and kissing him may scare him, and he may retreat into a shell. To open him up, to regain his trust, try to quiet his world. Calmly help him talk about what's on his mind.

For some children, the upheaval of their family by the

death of a parent or sibling may be aggravated by another major change, such as a move to another city. If it's at all possible, when there's a death in the family, try not to make another big change in routine right away. We may not be able to control the way we feel, but we can control how those feelings are expressed, how we make decisions, and how we handle ourselves and our lives. "I see this is a family thing," says bereavement counselor Gwen Schwartz-Borden. "When there's a death, I don't single the kids out and just counsel them on how to deal with it. It's a problem the whole family has to face."

Others May Disagree With Your Approach

As with many parenting decisions that you face over the years, the decision to talk with your children openly about death may be met by well-meaning friends and relatives trying to harpoon the whole idea. They might not believe in the kind of openness we've been talking about. "What do you mean, you're bringing him to the funeral? In our family we just don't do things like that!" "He's going to a movie on the day before his mother's funeral? I've never heard of such a thing!" "Did you see Jamie? He wasn't even wearing a suit and tie!"

My program is based on a relationship between parent and child in which the parent feels very strongly that the child is a person with a right to know what's happening around him, a right to get help in this time of crisis, and a right to express how he's feeling in his own way. Along with all these rights, the child also has a responsibility to do what he can to help the team, as it were—the family. But some people will try to stop your efforts, to resist your way of doing things, either with an all-out onslaught or subtle skirmishes.

Mimi sat in my office with her two elderly aunts, going

over the details of her father's funeral. When I asked her what she planned to say to her five-year-old, the two aunts broke in. "Oh, he doesn't know a thing! No need to tell him or bother him about all this." "Oh, yes, he needs to know!" Mimi asserted, and then we talked about what she would say to the child about his grandfather's death. All through our conversation, the two aunts muttered to each other about how ridiculous this all was. "Why upset the child?" Finally, Mimi stopped and glared at them. "He's going to be told and he's going to be part of the funeral!" she said.

Another family came in to see me with a thirteen-year-old. Brad was with his mother, father, grandmother, and Uncle Tom, who kept grumbling about how this kid should not be here. Finally, the whole group got up to go look at a casket, and Uncle Tom stopped Brad. "You can't come," he said. The child's reply: "Why not? I'm going to see it anyhow later on; why not now?" The boy went with his parents to help pick out the casket, with the uncle grudgingly going along.

Brad's uncle thought he was doing the right thing; so did Mimi's two aunts. Most relatives offering advice mean well, but they are not the child's parents. Only you as parents know what you want to say to your children, and in what kind of atmosphere you want to raise them.

One mother whose husband had died was advised by a dear friend, a rabbi, not to say anything to her five-year-old about his father's death. "He won't even remember his father three months from now." How do you respond to advice like that? I suggest that you explain where your values are on this. Say something like, "Listen, this is something that I believe is really important to this child and I must do it. I have to tell him the truth and let him be part of this funeral. Now, I'd really like your support. I'd love to have you help me out and I'll tell you what I'm saying to him. But please don't try to change it."

Finally, remember that most of these people will be with you for just a few days. You are the one who has to live with your child's questions.

Let Your Child Know What to Expect From Others

It's comforting to a child to know how different people in the family group will act when they're grieving. Take a good look at the family and describe to your child what he'll be seeing. "Aunt Sadie will probably get hysterical when she sees Grandpa. Uncle Ned will probably sit in the corner quietly and not talk with anyone." Also, prepare him for what people may say, so when he gets mixed messages he knows how to handle them. "Uncle Jim may tell you to be strong because men don't cry, but you'll see other men crying because that's what some people do when they feel sad."

Some people don't know how to talk to children as if they were people. The only way they can communicate is by telling fairy tales that blur the distinction in the youngster's mind between fact and fancy.

Tell your child that sometimes people feel so bad because a person died that they get a little confused. They think that not telling children what really happened—that telling a make-believe story—will make the children feel better and not miss the person who died. One mother I know told her five-year-old that this would happen. At the wake, her child came up to her. "Mommy, Uncle Bill just told me that Grandma is asleep and she'll be getting up later. He did that because he doesn't want me to feel bad, right?"

If the foundation is laid, your child will be better able to accept the negative aspects of the family support system. When Sean, the cool-headed teenager we met earlier in this chapter, was asked by a distraught aunt why he didn't seem very upset that Grandpa had died, he knew how to deal with the question. "I knew she was under a lot of stress so I didn't worry about it. I figured that's just the way she is."

Give Your Child the Opportunity to Participate and Help

Judy's husband died of cancer slowly, over the course of a year and a half. During that time, Dawn, their ten-year-old daughter, knew what was going on, helped out where she could, and grieved with her parents as her father died. There were no secrets. When the end finally came, Dawn was prepared. She was upset, but she had said her goodbyes, helped her father in his last days, and was able to handle her loss rather well.

The key to this kind of open communication, where a child is free to say what's on his mind and where he feels secure within his family, is a place for him within the support network. Let him be an active part of the group. Young children can answer the doorbell or go on errands; older children can help make funeral arrangements, answer the phone, or pick people up at the airport. Ask your child what he wants to do to help, and make sure he knows that you *need* that help. By being part of the system, he'll learn a lot—seeing how other people handle themselves, how they grieve. It will show him that he is able to handle difficult emotions and to help other people.

4.

The Funeral—Finding a Way to Say Goodbye

Several years ago, in a segment on the TV show "Different Strokes," the young leading character (played by Gary Coleman) asked to be taken to his mother's grave. As he sat by the tombstone, he poured out his feelings, apologizing to her many years after her death for never having said goodbye. "They wouldn't let me come to the funeral, they thought I was too young," he said. "They thought I wouldn't understand. So I had to come now." The child wanted to make sure that his mother knew he cared.

Scenes like that don't happen when parents include their children in the rituals our culture has provided for people to express their grief. Children, like adults, need a vehicle to mourn their loss, to say goodbye and get on with living again. Families deprived of this catharsis, because their loved ones were missing in action or lost at sea, often have a hard time coming to terms with the loss. Unless they are able to face the death squarely, acknowledge the loss in some kind of ritual and bury the one they loved, the grief doesn't go away. As sociologist Alvin Toffler points out in *Future Shock*, the funeral is an important change-buffer, marking off a significant event in our lives.

With the gathering of friends, the religious services, and perhaps a procession to the place of burial, the funeral gives people a ritual in which they can start to resolve their feelings about the death. It also gives them something to do. For many years it was felt that becoming involved in the funeral preparations only made the grief worse—so very often one person in the family, "the strong one," was expected to put his or her feelings on hold and handle all the arrangements. Others appeared only when they were told to come. All that is changing now, however. These preparations are now seen by many people as an outlet for grief and anxiety.

Parents I've talked to have found that not giving their children the choice of attending the funeral, in an attempt to protect them from pain, is a tactic that can often backfire.

It was winter in the upper midwest, and the snow lay in drifts around the college town. Debbie climbed through the snowbanks, up the steps of her dorm, and walked into the reception room. "Debbie," yelled a friend, "you got a message to call home immediately." Debbie called home; her father was dead. "I'm coming right now," she told her mother. It took nearly twenty-four hours on buses that got stuck in the blizzard, and on trains and planes, but finally she made it back to New York and walked in the door. "When's the funeral going to be?" she finally asked after the hugs and the tears. "I didn't want you to have to go through it," her mother said. "I had your father cremated this morning."

It's hard to fault that mother; she really felt that what she was doing was right. She meant well, but in the midst of the crisis she forgot that her daughter had the right to make a choice, too—to see her father before he was cremated if she wanted to.

Rabbi Earl Grollman, editor of the book *Explaining Death to Children*, says that for children the funeral service is a positive learning experience, one that helps them accept the reality of death as separation, even as they are taught about birth and maturity. "As a rite of passage, the funeral helps to instill the feeling in the child that he is part of the order of things."

Carol Smith-Torres, a chaplain at the Columbia Presbyterian Medical Center in New York City, points out that there are different ways of asking the question "Do you want to go to the funeral?", and each way sends a different message to the child.

First, you might say, "Do you really want to go?" That sends the message, "Don't come!"

Second, you might say, "You're coming to the funeral, aren't you?" That tells the child he'd better come.

Third, a parent can ask, "Would you like to come to the funeral with me?" That gives the youngster a choice.

Most people think that funerals are all alike, but the fact is that no two are ever alike. I know, because as a funeral director, I've been involved in thousands of them. Just as people are different and families are different, so are the ways they say goodbye to their loved ones.

Reverend Doug Manning, in *A Minister Speaks About Funerals*, suggests that within each funeral, the family should have a "private time," an hour or so in which they sit down as a group and swap stories about the one they loved. It's much like the Jewish custom of "sitting shiva." When a person dies, it matters to the other family members that his or her life had significance. In this private time, the family deals with this significance, relating stories about how the dead person touched their lives. It gives everyone a license to discuss both the good times and the bad. While they're sitting there, the children will learn how to handle themselves in their grief; they'll see that it's okay to express negative feelings or even to laugh in the midst of grief.

TELLING CHILDREN WHAT TO EXPECT

Should children be allowed to come to the funeral home? Definitely—but they must be prepared first about what to expect. Whether they're preschoolers or teenagers, whether they're self-possessed or timid, they should be carefully schooled on what they'll be seeing. Then they can make an informed choice about whether to go to the funeral home or not. Walking in cold on a situation you've never experienced before—especially a scene charged with this kind of emotion— can be terribly unnerving.

Many hospital personnel realize the importance of preparing children for what to expect. Several years ago, my youngest son went in for surgery. On the day he went into the hospital, we were taken on a tour of the operating room and intensive care, the recovery room, and the room where he'd be staying. A nurse showed him how she gives injections by using a doll; he was given a face mask to play jet pilot with so he wouldn't be alarmed when it came time for the anesthesia; the whole experience was made very familiar to him. Later, as each procedure was performed, there were no surprises.

I propose that the same consideration be given to a child coming to a funeral. No matter what age he is, the youngster should be told what to expect—the size of the room, the fact that there may be a lot of flowers, who will be coming and how they will probably be dressed, how long the child will stay, when he must leave, and why. (Adults need some time for themselves.)

To a young child you might say something like: "Grandpa's going to be in a big room with a green rug and yellow wallpaper, and there will be paintings on the wall and lots of flowers around the casket. Grandpa will be lying down in the casket, which is a box that they bury Grandpa in so that no dirt gets on him [this is important to many children]. Grandpa's casket is silver and he's dressed in his dark blue suit, and he'll be lying down and not moving, because his body doesn't work anymore. He'll still look the same—just very still. When we go in, a lot of people will be standing and sitting around and some of them will be crying because they're so sad that Grandpa died. And if you want to, you can come in the room where Grandpa will be and say a prayer or say goodbye to Grandpa. He won't be able to hear you because his body isn't working, but if there's something special that you want to leave in the casket with Grandpa, a flower or something, you can do that."

As always, you must change this explanation to fit your particular family customs and religious traditions. The important thing is that the experience should be described as fully as possible.

The message must be structured very carefully—never assume that your child understands what you do. One little boy was given a very detailed explanation of how Grandpa's body would be brought from the hospital to the funeral home. Then he was asked, "Do you want to go to the funeral home to see Grandpa?" "No," the child replied. "How come?" "I don't want to see Grandpa without his arms and legs and head." Where did he ever get such an idea? "Well, when Mommy gives me a bath, she tells me to wash my arms and legs and head, and then wash my body, and Daddy said they were bringing Grandpa's *body* to the funeral home."

Many people, when they hear that story, are surprised that a child would have that reaction. But such misunderstandings are common. When you're talking about the dead person, use his or her name, not the word "body." Don't assume that a child knows that when a body is in a casket, it's lying down. One youngster came into the funeral home and got very upset because Grandpa wasn't sitting up like he was the last time he saw him. Don't assume, either, that children know that a dead body doesn't move or that a person really is inside the casket when it's closed. Children often believe only what they see, and if they see only the head and torso of the body, they often think the other half is missing or that the body is a fake. It is important to confront this issue gently. I suggest saying to your child, "Some children think that only half a person is there—if you want, we can have the funeral director open the bottom half and show you his legs. . . ." Let them touch the dead person if they want to.

One young fellow pulled up his father's sleeve, saw his tattoo and said, "That's Daddy, all right!" Eighty-five percent of the children I ask say yes, they do want to have the casket opened all the way so they can see that the lower half of the body is there. It's better than letting their imaginations go wild.

As I've said, the child should be given a choice, after the explanations have been made, as to whether he wants to go to the funeral home, the funeral service, and/or the cemetery. Never force him to go to any of them. Also, never push him into doing something he doesn't want to do, such as walking up and touching the body at the funeral home, even if everyone else is doing it. Always allow him to change his mind, even at the last minute.

If your child doesn't want to go to the service, try to get him or her to talk about it. Sometimes they have their reasons. Elizabeth said she didn't want to have as the last image in her mind a grandfather who was dead—she wanted to remember him as he was when she last saw him, playing baseball with the kids in the park. That was her choice and it should be respected. But if your children want to come and say goodbye, they should be given that right, too.

Children often handle their crises better than we adults do, when they're equipped with the right information. Even a child of four or five, if he has a certain amount of self-discipline, should be allowed to come to the funeral home for a short visit, if he wants to. Children in the early school years can be expected to sit quietly for up to half an hour. Parents can ask that a special time be set aside for young children to visit the funeral home—so that they can avoid the busy times and be able to devote themselves to answering their children's questions. Especially if the person who died is their parent, young children should be allowed to see the dead person for a moment or two, because unless they have some memory of the body at the funeral they may have trouble believing that their loved one is actually dead.

It's important, though, not to leave the child alone by the casket to fend for himself. Dr. Hal Fishkin remembers going to the funeral home to see a friend who died. When he walked in he asked where his friend's sixteen-year-old son was. "Oh, he's in there with his mother," Fishkin was told. The boy had been sitting beside his dead mother for half an hour and no one had wanted to disturb him. "I walked in and the boy was sitting there. So I said to him, 'Come on, let's go.' And he came along. He was glad that someone had come in and told him to leave." Children need to be told what to do sometimes. When they're upset, they need someone to help them get themselves back together.

If a child is surrounded by sensible adults and allowed to talk out his feelings, he'll usually handle the time at the funeral home just fine. Very often he'll find the ritual fascinating, learn from the experience, and come out of it feeling supported, part of the group. The adults are the ones who set the limits and control what is going to happen in this crisis. If the adults behave honestly, calmly, and lovingly, the children will respond in kind.

THE SPECIAL GESTURE

Many parents I've worked with have found that a "goodbye gift" is an effective way to help their child realize the finality of death, and perform one last act of recognition and respect. I suggest to parents that when they're making funeral arrangements they let their children order the kind of flowers Grandma would have liked, or choose some of the music. Some youngsters make a last gift to be put in the casket—a drawing or a letter saying goodbye, telling how they loved the person who died. I've had little kids pull dandelions out of the backyard and stick them in Grandpa's hand in the casket. They may have looked like weeds to us, but to the little ones they were something significant . . . an appropriate way to say "I love you." Make sure, though, that the child who writes a letter or puts a gift in the casket knows that the dead person can't read or see or use the present.

A youngster needs a license to do what he thinks is best when he's saying goodbye. One thirteen-year-old boy, whose grandfather was his baseball coach, put his prized baseball trophy in the casket. Many members of the family thought that was a terrible idea, but the boy's parents went along with his wish. They pointed out to him that there was no getting it back; but if that's what he wanted, it was okay with them. They acknowledged him and accepted his decision.

Sometimes children and adults need to keep something that reminds them of the one they loved. When a family refuses to move anything out of the dead person's room—to keep it as a shrine—that can be dangerous, an unhealthy form of bonding in an attempt to idealize the dead person. But keeping a little remembrance can be a good thing.

Mark Oberman wrote an article for *Newsday Magazine* about what it was like when his infant son died. In the story, he described how his father had "stolen" a pair of the child's sneakers and kept them alongside his own shoes on the floor of his closet. Finally, the father gave his son one of the sneakers. "Since we made that poignant exchange, I, too, keep that one little blue sneaker on the floor of my clothes closet along with my shoes. Somehow, it gives me great comfort. It helps me, in a small way, to accept his life and his death. To enjoy the child in me. To live more fully in the present."

Some parents arrange for the children to have their own little service, which the children plan themselves and to which they invite whoever they like. This is often a good time to answer questions and straighten out misconceptions. One little boy who was told that Grandpa can now see God in heaven thought that Grandpa's body may be here, but his eyes were in heaven. Another got really upset that Grandma was being buried in the ground. "Isn't it cold down there?" His parents returned to their explanation of what "dead" means and said that Grandma couldn't be cold because her body had stopped working and she couldn't feel anything anymore. Talking it out gives them a chance to verbalize their feelings and absorb the shock of the death.

QUESTIONS YOUR CHILD MIGHT ASK

The older a child gets, the more questions a parent may have to answer.

- "Do they drain the blood out before they put a body in the casket?"
- "How did they make him look so real?" (Implying that the body lying in the casket is a fake.)

Preteens and teenagers will often be interested in the mechanics surrounding the funeral. Here are a series of questions and answers that might help.

Q: Why is the body embalmed?
A: Unless the body is embalmed immediately, it will decompose very quickly. So certain chemicals are injected into the body, like a transfusion. The body is cleaned and the hair is washed. The openings of the body are disinfected and closed so that none of the fluids will come out. The parts of the body that were damaged are specially treated and restored.

Q: Why can't they leave the person's body alone when they die? Why do they have to put make-up on him and make him look phoney?
A: If the body disintegrated through disease or was in a violent death, the funeral preparation tries to fix up those scars so people won't see the dead person looking so bad. No one's trying to deny that the person died; the people at the funeral home just try to make the dead person look like he did when he was alive, so his loved ones will have a nicer image to remember. [Some say this is denying death—but the greatest denial is a closed casket.]

Q: What is cremation?
A: The body is put into intense heat and turned into ashes. Sometimes the ashes are put in an urn, sometimes they're buried, and sometimes they're scattered over the ground or the ocean.

Q: What is a wake?
A: Before a person is buried, many people like to get together and talk about the dead person while the body is present. It's also called "calling hours."

Q: Why do people send flowers? It's a waste; the dead person can't see them.
A: The family of the person who died can look at the flowers and see that the person was important to a lot of folks. Some people, instead of flowers, send a donation to the person's favorite charity.

After a child has the answers to his questions, he'll probably want to know how to act at the funeral. Perhaps a friend of the family or a schoolmate died. Explain that when he goes to visit the family at the funeral home, he should just be himself. It's not necessary to say much. Whatever you do say, the more personal and heartfelt, the better. Tell the child if he wants to talk about things he remembers about the dead person, that would be fine. Or he might even talk about how sad he feels or angry that the person died; that will let the family know how much he cares. Let him know that if he feels like crying, that's okay. Knowing that other people are grieving too lightens the load. And just being a good listener can do a world of good.

When we talk about death, we get in touch with life. Sometimes in our day-to-day routine we get so caught up in doing things that we forget what's really important . . . our beliefs, our dreams, the ones we love. But when we talk about death and, for a moment, confront the fact that no one's going to live forever, that we're only here for a little while, we strip away the trappings of our lives and get to the core of what we feel and believe. We become more human as we realize how precious it is to be alive. How wonderful it is if we can share that moment with our children!

Crisis Section

This section is intended to serve as a quick reference to the information given in more detail throughout the book. Here you will find, in outline form, the parts of the "message" that you want to send to your children. As I said before, not everything here will apply to your particular situation; you will have to pick and choose from the information offered here. Remember also that although this material is directed toward explaining the death of a person, you can take a similar approach when you're explaining the death of a pet.

I hope that this section will prove useful to you during a crisis, or any time you need a ready answer to a specific question or situation, and that you will also refer back to the first four chapters for more of this information and the impact it can have on your children. Few people in crisis will have the energy to read the whole book at that time; understanding this and, at the same time, acknowledging your own need will help you help your children.

When you confront the problem of telling your children about the death,

1. Accept that it's not easy. You may:

    - *be upset and stressed*
    - *lack energy*
    - *feel unable to concentrate*
    - *worry about how your emotions will affect your child*
    - *be concerned about the effect of the death on your child*
    - *want to protect your child from pain*
    - *not know how much your child understands about death*

2. Be prepared for resistance from others. People may say of your children:

    - *They don't know what's going on.*
    - *Wait until later to tell them.*
    - *Make up a story.*
    - *Don't say anything.*
    - *Send them away until the funeral is over.*
    - *Why do you want to put them through this?*

    Consider saying to these people:

    - *I really could use your help; I believe that what I am doing is the right thing for my children and me.*
    - *You can help me by reinforcing what I am telling them, or by saying nothing. Don't undermine my effort.*

    Parents should know that children will:

    - *read emotions around them*
    - *respond to body language*
    - *overhear conversations*
    - *ask questions directly or indirectly.*

Your children will receive some kind of message, no matter what you do; *it is impossible not to communicate.* They will see your grief and if you have not explained what's going on, it will signal to them that something is the matter. They will be confused and anxious.

Control the message instead by giving them accurate information, geared for the age of the child, in language he or she can understand.

UNDERSTANDING SADNESS

1. Your children need to know:

   - *why you are sad*
   - *why others are sad*
   - *why they are sad.*

   Acknowledging this lets your children know that it's *okay* to be sad. Tell them, "This is how we feel when someone dies."

2. Children must be told that it is the death that has made you sad. Without an explanation, they may think your sadness is caused by something they did or didn't do. Start by saying:

   - *"This is a very, very sad time . . ."*
   - *"A very, very sad thing has happened . . ."*
   - *"Mommy and Daddy are sad because . . ."*

UNDERSTANDING "DEAD" AND WHAT IT MEANS

1. Explain that *dead* means that:

   - *A person's body has stopped working and won't work anymore.*
   - *The body won't do any of the things it used to do: it won't talk, walk, move, see, or hear; none of the parts work.*
   - *The person won't feel any of the feelings he or she used to feel, such as sad, mad, happy, hurt, hot, or cold.*
   - *The person will not eat, drink, or go to the bathroom (urinate and defecate) anymore.*

2. Refer back to this explanation when answering questions that arise, such as:

   - *Will Grandpa ever move again? (No, his body has stopped working.)*
   - *Why can't they fix him? (Once the body stops working, it can't start again.)*
   - *Why is he cold? (The body only stays warm when it's working, like ours.)*
   - *Why isn't he moving? (He can't move because his body isn't working any more.)*
   - *When will he come back? (He won't. People who die don't come back.)*
   - *Is he sleeping? (No. When we sleep our body is still working, just resting.)*
   - *Can he hear me? (No. He could only hear you if his body was working.)*
   - *Can he eat after he's buried? (No, a person eats only when his body is working.)*

3. Don't use words like "passed away," "left us," "gone on"; to a child this sounds like the person is taking a trip. His

parents' trips may then become a source of anxiety, if the child thinks that some people never return from them. Don't hold out any hope of return; death is a form of abandonment.

SPECIAL CHARACTERISTICS TO KEEP IN MIND

NEWBORN TO AGE THREE

1. No matter how young the child, he or she can sense when things in the family routine are different. However, they will not be able to figure out why they are different. Among the changes in the daily routine that children might sense are:

   - *excitement at home*
   - *sadness or anxiety*
   - *presence of new people*
   - *parents being gone at odd times*
   - *a significant person in their lives is missing*

2. Watch your child to see if he or she starts acting differently. Among the changes you might note are:

   - *stopped or altered nursing patterns (in infants)*
   - *crankiness*
   - *altered sleep patterns*
   - *change in eating habits*

3. Children in this age group cannot comprehend the concept of death; however, they can understand sadness. When you know what changes to look for in your children, you can respond more sensitively to their needs.

AGE THREE TO SIX

1. Children in this age group think death is reversible: people will come back; death isn't forever. E.T. came back from the dead; also Jesus and Lazarus. The coyote on the Roadrunner cartoon program gets right back up again after being squashed.

   They will ask questions about the dead person's return; also, they may not be really affected by the death, since they expect the person to come back soon. They cannot understand the concept of "finality" at this age.

2. They will connect events that don't belong connected:

   - *Does this mean someone else is going to die?*
   - *Grandpa died from a headache; Mommy says she has a headache too . . .*
   - *Old people die; Daddy is very old; Daddy may die too . . .*

   Be prepared for indirect questions, aimed at finding out if someone else might die: "How old are you? How old is Daddy?"

   You must explain the difference between:

   - *very, very sick and just "sick"*
   - *very, very old and over 20*
   - *very old and very sick, and very old and not sick*

3. It's important that your child not assume he is responsible in any way for the death. See page 131 of the crisis section.

4. Explain about the emotions your child may be feeling or observing:

   - *Crying is okay for everyone (boys, too).*
   - *Feeling bad inside is okay. After a while, you'll feel better.*

- *Being mad is okay.*
- *People in the family might have trouble sleeping or eating; this is a natural reaction.*

AGE SIX TO NINE

1. Most children in this age group will understand that death is final; but some might still think that the dead person will come back.

2. Children in this age group need a more detailed explanation of why the person died. It's important to distinguish fatal illness from just being sick ("It's not like when your stomach hurts, or when Mommy gets a cold . . ."). They may have a greater fear of their parents' dying, particularly if they see them as vulnerable (often ill, etc.). This concern is even greater when they are being raised by a single parent.

3. They see death as a taker; something that comes and gets you. Or they may see it as something you catch, like a cold. They also may not want to go to a house where someone has died.

4. Explain about the emotions your child may be feeling or observing:

   - *Crying is okay for everyone (boys, too).*
   - *Feeling bad is okay.*
   - *Feeling frightened is okay.*
   - *Being angry is okay.*
   - *Feeling that something is missing is okay.*

Parents often find it helpful to share some of their own feelings with their children; it helps start discussion.

5. Because children in this age group connect death with violence, they may ask when being told about a death, "Who killed him?"

6. Make sure your child does not feel responsible for the death in any way; see page 131 of the crisis section.

AGE NINE TO TWELVE

1. Children in this age group are more aware of the finality of death and of the impact that a death may have on them—even to the point where it affects family security and economic security.

   These feelings are quite close to those experienced by adults, and parents say it helps to share their own thoughts and feelings with their children.

2. Children may show more anger, guilt, and grief. See pages 129–132 in the crisis section.

TEENAGERS

1. The older your children, the greater the temptation to assume they can handle themselves and their problems. *Don't assume this*; they need your help and support to understand their feelings at this time.

   Check especially pages 129–132 in the crisis section.

DESCRIBING HOW/WHY THE DEATH OCCURRED (TO YOUNG CHILDREN)

1. Old Age

   - *"When a person gets very, very, very old, his body wears out and stops working . . ."*

2. Terminal Illness

- *"Because the disease couldn't be stopped, the person got very, very sick; his body wore out and stopped working . . ."*

3. Accident

- *"A terrible thing happened (car crash, etc.); his body was badly hurt and couldn't be fixed. It stopped working . . ."*

4. Miscarriage

- *"Sometimes when a baby is just starting to grow, something happens that makes it stop. We don't know what it was; it wasn't anything anyone did . . ."*

5. Stillborn

- *"Sometimes something makes a baby die before it is born. We're not sure why, but it's nothing anybody did or didn't do . . ."*

6. Sudden Infant Death Syndrome (SIDS)

- *"Sometimes with little babies something makes their bodies stop working. It's nothing anybody did or forgot to do. Doctors are not sure why it happens . . ."*

7. Suicide—Absolute (when there is no doubt the person killed himself)

- *"Some people's bodies get sick and just don't work right; and sometimes a person's mind doesn't work right. They can't see things clearly and they feel the only way to solve their problems is to take their lives—to kill themselves. However, this is never a solution to problems; they only reason they thought of it is that they weren't thinking very clearly . . ."*

8. Suicide—Questionable

- *"Sometimes people take pills to relax or to sleep. Sometimes they forget how many they took and think they need more. These pills make a person's body slow down. Too many of them make the body stop working. We don't think the person wanted to die, but that's what happened . . ."*

9. Homicide

- *"Sometimes very bad people do very bad things . . ."*

AFTER THE DEATH—WHAT WILL HAPPEN NOW

1. Children should be told what is going to happen and what they are going to experience. Should they be brought to the funeral home and/or service? Definitely—if they are well prepared in advance. Tell them what will happen, then give them the choice of going or not. Fit the following explanation around your family's plans and special traditions:

   "_____ will be taken from _____, where he died, to the funeral home. At the funeral home _____ will be dressed in clothes that he liked and put into a casket. A casket is a box we use so that when _____ is buried, no dirt will get on him. Because _____'s body isn't working any more, it won't move or do any of the things it used to do. But it will look like _____ always did.

   People will come and visit us and say how sorry they are that _____ died. After _____ days the casket will be closed and taken to church, where people will say prayers for _____. Then we will go to the cemetery, where _____ will be buried in a place that _____ picked out.

If you like, you can come to the funeral home and visit for a while—even go to the cemetery. You could bring something to leave with _____ if you want; that would be nice.

We have to go to the funeral home to make plans, and we'll let you know all about them when we come back. We will be gone _____ hours."

For a cremation, use this additional information:

"After we leave the funeral home, _____ will be taken to a crematory, a place where his body will be turned into ashes. Then we will take those ashes and _____ (scatter them; keep them in an urn). Since _____'s body doesn't work and doesn't feel anything, being cremated doesn't hurt."

If the dead person has changed because of illness or accident, it's important to describe some of this change. ("It's still Grandpa, but you know he was sick and lost a lot of weight—so he will look thinner . . .")

2. Describe the room in the funeral home where the person will be. Be very detailed and specific for younger children.

- *color of rug*
- *color of walls*
- *whether there are plants and paintings*
- *where the casket will be*
- *color and type of casket (wood, metal)*
- *color of the suit and tie, or dress, that the person will be wearing*
- *color of flowers*

3. Explain that the person will be

- *lying down*
- *not moving*
- *whether the whole body will be visible or not*

If you plan to have a closed casket, when possible I suggest the children be allowed to briefly look at the whole body so they'll realize that the person is, in fact, dead and in the casket. If the casket is going to be half open, children may think that only half of the person is there; show them that this is not so. You might say, "Some children think that only half of the person is there—so if you want, we can ask the funeral director to open the bottom and show you his legs." When there is a full open casket, children will see the whole person and know that he or she is there.

4. Ask your child whether he or she wants to come to the service or not. Some children do; others don't. Remember that:

- *If a child is left out there is no next time/no going back*
- *The child remembers not being able to say goodbye; not being included; not being given the choice.*

Telling a child what is happening and making him part of things, or asking him if he wants to be a part of things, draws him in. He makes the decision.

HOW CHILDREN MAY REACT

Children may

- *be very upset, picking up on the family's emotion*
- *be upset about not knowing what is happening*
- *not be upset at all; or be upset only for a little while (they may think that the person will be dead only for a time, then come back)*
- *act out difficult behaviors*
- *seek attention*
- *sulk or withdraw*
- *become angry or hostile*
- *not want to believe the person is dead*
- *not want to go to the funeral, which would confirm the death*
- *not want to talk about it*
- *want to join the deceased (suicide)*
- *romanticize the death*

ANGER

Anger is common at the time of a death; it can be very damaging to the family. Understanding it and anticipating it helps parents deal with both their own and their children's anger.

Children may be angry at their parents for:

- *not telling them that the person who died was so sick*
- *spending so much time with the sick person*
- *just because they need someone to be angry with*

Children may be angry at themselves for:

- *not intervening earlier (not taking the car keys away before an accident, etc.)*

- *wishing the person would die*
- *not visiting or helping the dying person*
- *not saying goodbye, or "I love you"*

Children may be angry at others for:

- *not taking care of the person who died (the bartender for serving him drinks; the doctors for not treating him adequately)*
- *hurting or killing the person (in the case of an accident or homicide)*

Children may be angry at the person who died for:

- *not taking care of himself or putting himself in danger*
- *leaving, dying, abandoning them*
- *causing such family upset*
- *using up the family money*
- *not telling anyone he was sick*
- *committing suicide (causing the family pain and stigma)*
- *not fighting harder against death*

Children may be angry at their brothers and sisters for:

- *no apparent reason*
- *grieving differently (some children cry, others don't)*
- *not seeming to care*
- *not wanting to talk about the death*
- *seeming more privileged (others can go to the funeral, but they can't)*

GUILT

Many people feel guilt about a death. This might stem from anger—

- *How can I be angry at the person who died?*
- *How can I be alive when he's dead?*

From the feeling that you didn't do enough—

- *I should have told the rest of the family that he was sick.*
- *I should have visited him before he died.*

And from all the "shouldn't haves"—

- *I shouldn't have left the hospital.*
- *I shouldn't have let him drive.*
- *I shouldn't have left him alone (suicide).*

RESPONSIBILITY

Guilt and a feeling of responsibility go hand-in-hand. Children can feel responsible for a person's death for a number of reasons:

- *They may have been told something that they misunderstood and took to heart ("you're driving me crazy"; "you'll be the death of me yet"; "you're killing your father").*
- *Because they often see God as a rewarder or punisher, they may feel God has punished their bad behavior by causing the person's death; also they may feel if they had prayed harder the person wouldn't have died.*
- *They connect events that don't belong together ("If I had sent a 'get well' card maybe he wouldn't have died").*
- *They indulge in magical thinking ("If I wish hard enough, he'll come back"; "I got mad and wished that he would die").*

This is why it is so important that children understand why the person died. Remember, your child may think he is responsible for the death, and tell him this is not so.

In the case of *actual* responsibility for a death—parents cannot make a child believe what he or she knows to be false; parents of children directly responsible for the death of another should strongly consider professional help.

Bibliography and
Support Groups

REFERENCES

Bergson, Lisa. "Suicide's Other Victims." *The New York Times*, 1982. Reprinted by the New York State Funeral Directors Association, Inc.

Bowlby, John. *Attachments, Separation, and Loss.* New York: Basic Books, 1969–1981.

Brody, Jane E. "The Haunting Spectre of Teenage Suicide." *The New York Times*, 1984. Reprinted by the New York State Funeral Directors Association, Inc.

Callahan, Dolores. "A Piece of the Whole." *Thanatos.* Volume 8, No. 2, Summer 1983.

De Bernardo, Francis. "Death of a Teacher Brings Awareness of Life, Love, and Pain." *The Tablet*, Dec. 17, 1983.

Elliott, Barbara. "Neonatal Death: Reflections for Parents." *Pediatrics.* Volume 62, 1978.

Furman, Erna. "The Death of a Newborn: Care of the Parents." *Birth and the Family Journal.* Vol. 5: 4 Winter 1978.

Grollman, Earl. *Explaining Death to Children.* Boston, Massachusetts: Beacon Press, 1967.

Klass, Dennis, and Gordon, Audrey. *They Need to Know.* Englewood Cliffs, New Jersey: Prentice-Hall, 1979.

Klein, Carole. *How It Feels to Be a Child.* New York: Harper & Row, 1977.

Krementz, Jill. *How It Feels When A Parent Dies.* New York: Alfred Knopf, 1981.

Kushner, Harold. *When Bad Things Happen to Good People.* New York: Avon Books, 1981.

Lefebvre, Leo C. "Sudden Infant Death Syndrome: Its Impact on Parents, Grandparents, Neighbors and Friends—From a Father's Perspective." Davenport, Iowa: Council of Guilds for Infant Survival, n.d.

Lindeman, Erich. "Symptomatology and Management of Acute Grief." Report to the Centenary Meeting of the American Psychiatric Association, Philadelphia, Pennsylvania, May 15–18, 1944.

Longpré, Elise. "It Seems So Long Ago." *Thanatos.* Volume 8, Number 2, Summer 1983.

Mandell, Frederick; McAnulty, Elizabeth S.; and Carlson, Andrew. "Unexpected Death of an Infant Sibling, study conducted at Children's Hospital Medical Center, Boston, Massachusetts." *Pediatrics.* Volume 72, Nov. 5, 1983.

Manning, Doug. *A Minister Speaks About Funerals*. Hereford, Texas: In-Light Books, 1978.

Oberman, Mark. "A Father's Lament: My Last 'Jewel.' " *Newsday*, May 22, 1983.

Patterson, Paul. Quoted in "Child and Death Perspectives from Birth Through Adolescence." *Archives of the Foundation of Thanatology*. Volume 10, Number 1.

Pynoos, Robert S. Quoted in "When Kids Witness a Parent's Death." Newsletter of the New York State Funeral Directors Association, January 1984.

Quirk, Tina Russo. "Crisis Theory, Grief Theory, and Related Psychosocial Factors; The Framework for Intervention." The Perinatal Bereavement Crisis Series. *Journal of Nurse-Midwifery*. Volume 24, Number 5, September-October 1979.

Satir, Virginia. *Peoplemaking*. Palo Alto, California: Science and Behavior Books, Inc., 1972.

Snyder, Barbara. *The Buffalo News*, Jan. 5, 1982. Reprinted in *Thanatos*. Volume 8, Number 2.

Toffler, Alvin. *Future Shock*. New York: Random House, 1970.

Turkington, Carol. "Support Urged for Children in Mourning." *Monitor*. December 1984.

Typond, Claudia. "The Death of a Child: A Case Study." *Archives of Thanatology*. Volume 10, Number 1.

Wanzenreid, John. "What to Say to SIDS Parents." Reprinted by the New York State Funeral Directors Association.

SUGGESTIONS FOR FURTHER READING

The following list was prepared by Roberta Halporn, M.A., Director of the Center for Thanatology Research and Educa-

*tion. All of the publications in this list may be ordered from
the Center. A full bibliography may be obtained by sending a
stamped, self-addressed Number 10 envelope to 391 Atlantic
Avenue, Brooklyn, N.Y. 11217.*

For Adults

General

Feifel, Herman. *The Meaning of Death.* New York: McGraw-
Hill, 1959. Philosophical overview of American attitudes
toward death.

Grollman, Earl. *Concerning Death.* Boston, Massachusetts:
Beacon Press, 1974. A more general approach.

Kübler-Ross, Elisabeth. *On Death and Dying.* New York:
Macmillan, 1969. The best-known statement by a medical
doctor on how denying death works in the American medical
complex.

Children's Conceptions of Death

Cook, Sarah Sheets. *Children and Dying, An Exploration
and Annotated Bibliography.* New York: Center for Thanatology Research and Education, 1974. Short essays that
cover children's ideas, from kindergarten to adolescence.

Gullo, Steven V.; Patterson, Paul R.; and Schowalter, John
E., et. al., editors. *Death and Children: A Guide for
Educators, Parents, and Caregivers.* Dobbs Ferry, New York:
Tappan Press, 1985. A wide-ranging anthology, by educators
and psychologists with long-term experience.

Lonetto, Richard. *Children's Conceptions of Death.* New
York: Springer, 1980. A more academic, in-depth study.

Working with Children

Grollman, Earl. *Explaining Death to Children*. Boston, Massachusetts: Beacon Press, 1976. A thoughtful text that takes the mystery out of a very difficult topic.

Jewett, Claudia L., and Hadley, S. *Helping Children Cope with Separation and Loss*. Massachusetts: Bergin & Garvey Pubs., Inc., 1982. Relates the smaller issues of everyday loss to the loss of an intimate because of death.

On the Death of an Infant

Berg, Susan, and Lasker, Judith. *When Pregnancy Fails: Families Coping with Miscarriage, Still-birth, and Infant Death*. Boston, Massachusetts: Beacon Press, 1981. Two parents who lost children apply their perspective to a personal loss.

Johnson, Joy and Marv. *Children Die, Too*. Omaha, Nebraska: Centering Corp., 1978. A short pamphlet to be used during the initial shock of learning that a child might die.

Loss of a Parent

Furman, Erna. *A Child's Parent Dies*. New Haven, Connecticut: Yale University Press, 1974. An in-depth study of the long term results, by an eminent psychologist.

On Suicide

Bolton, Iris, and Mitchell, Curtis. *My Son, My Son: Healing After a Suicide*. Augusta, Georgia: Bolton Press, 1983. Group techniques for grieving parents.

Giffen, Mary, and Felsenthal, Carol. *A Cry for Help*. New York: Doubleday and Co., 1983. How to read the warning signs in teenagers.

Madison, Arnold. *Suicide and Young People*. New York: Clarion Press, 1978. A brief discussion of what is known about self-harm, and some prevention techniques.

On Funerals

Consumer Reports editors. *Funerals: Consumers' Last Rights*. New York: Random House, 1977. A complete analysis of the options available by the reputed consumer protection group.

Irion, Paul. *The Funeral: Vestige or Value*. Milwaukee, Wisconsin: Bulfin Press, 1971. An analysis of the positive and negative aspects of traditional rites.

For Children

General

Berger, Terry. *I Have Feelings*. New York: Human Sciences Press, 1971. An illustrated explanation for the 4- to 8-year-old that ugly feelings are as valid as beautiful ones.

Bernstein, Joanne. *Loss and How to Cope with It*. New York: Seabury Press, 1977. A straightforward address, in language suitable for the middle schooler.

Miles, Miska. *Annie and the Old One*. Boston, Massachusetts: Houghton Mifflin, 1971. A much-beloved fictional classic recounting an Indian grandmother's explanation of death to a young child. (8–12 years)

Stein, Sarah Bonnett. *About Dying: An Open Family Book for Parent and Child*. New York: Walker & Co., 1974. A beautifully illustrated book for parent and child, explaining the role of death in the life cycle. (3–6 years)

White, E. B. *Charlotte's Web*. New York: Harper & Row, 1952. A fictional classic of a little spider's courage. (5 years up)

Williams, Margery. *The Velveteen Rabbit*. Boston, Massachusetts: David Godine, 1956. A fairy tale about a manufactured pet rabbit, who becomes so old he gets lost to his youthful master. (Kindergarten)

About Aging

Blue, Rose. *Grandma Didn't Wave Back*. New York: Dell, 1972. Explaining the changes in a beloved grandmother's personality. (7–10 years)

De Paola, Tomie. *Nana Upstairs, Nana Downstairs*. New York: Putnam, 1973. When grandma "upstairs" finally dies, grandma "downstairs" is now old enough to take her place. (Kindergarten–7 years)

Fassler, Joan. *My Grandpa Died Today*. New York: Human Sciences Press, 1971. Recalling the sweetness of the child's relationship with grandpa before his death. (6–10 years)

On the Funeral

Johnson, Joy and Marv. *Tell Me Papa. Tell Me About Death and Funerals*. Omaha, Nebraska: Centering Corp., 1978. A graphic book, with soft wash illustrations, which shows what it looks like at the funeral and at the graveside. (6–10 years)

Viorst, Judith. *The Tenth Good Thing About Barney*. New York: Atheneum, 1971. A more euphemistic story about burying a beloved cat under a tree in the garden. (6–9 years)

Loss of a Parent

Hammond, Janice. *When My Daddy Died and When Mommy Died*. Cincinnati, Ohio: Cranbrook Press, 1981.

Simple drawings and text for the very young child. (4 years up)

Krementz, Jill. *How It Feels When a Parent Dies*. New York: Random House, 1981. A series of photo-essays by a noted photographer, with descriptions in the childrens' own words. (9–12 years)

Le Shan, Eda. *Learning to Say Goodbye: When a Parent Dies*. New York: Macmillan, 1976. A gentle explanation by a psychologist. (8–10 years)

Loss of a Sibling

Johnson, Joy and Marv. *Where's Jess?* Omaha, Nebraska: Centering Corp., 1982. A charmingly rendered set of answers to a little girl's questions about what has happened to her baby sister. (3–5 years)

Lee, Virginia. *The Magic Moth*. New York: Seabury Press, 1972. A fictional classic of terminal illness and death, seen through the eyes of a young brother. (8–11 years)

Levy, Erin Linn. *Children Are Not Paper Dolls*. Barrington, Illinois: The Publishers Mark, 1982. A coloring book for children ages 6 up that can help them express their feelings of grief and anger when a brother or sister dies.

For Adolescents

Craven, Margaret. *I Heard the Owl Call My Name*. New York: Dell, 1973. A young priest learns from the Alaskan Indians he serves how to regard his own life and death. (Fiction)

Gunther, John. *Death Be Not Proud*. New York: Harper &

row, 1971. A beautifully written account of a teenager's decline from a brain tumor; book is still much beloved. (Non-fiction)

Lund, Doris. *Eric*. New York: Dell, 1974. How Eric lived to the fullest before he died, described by his mother. (Non-fiction)

Re-Marriage

Green, Phyllis. *A New Mother for Martha*. New York: Human Sciences Press, 1978. Martha creates a shrine to her dead mother at home and resents the presence of a new woman in the house. (Fiction)

SUPPORT GROUPS

The Candlelighters. 123 C St. S.E., Washington, D.C. 20003. For parents of children with cancer.

The Compassionate Friends. P.O. Box 1347. Oak Brook, Illinois 60521. For parents whose children have died.

Mothers Against Drunk Drivers (MADD). 5330 Primrose, Suite 146. Fair Oaks, California 95628.

National Sudden Infant Death Foundation. 310 S. Michigan Ave., Chicago, Illinois 60604. Conducts research, offers preventive assistance, and aids the bereaved.

Parents of Murdered Children. 1739 Bella Vista, Cincinnati, Ohio 45237.

Index

About the Authors

DAN SCHAEFER is director of the funeral home in Brooklyn, New York, founded by his great-grandfather in 1878. A member of the professional advisory board of the Foundation of Thanatology at Columbia Presbyterian Medical Center, he is a guest lecturer to students of the College of Physicians and Surgeons of Columbia University, and to students at the School of Nursing of Columbia University. He has also participated in numerous symposia and workshops on coping with death and dying. He lives in Malverne, New York.

CHRISTINE LYONS is a journalist and reporter whose work has appeared in *The New York Times* and *The New York Post*, among other publications. She lives in New York City.

Other Parenting and Child Care Books
Available from Newmarket Press

Baby Massage
Parent-Child Bonding Through Touching
Amelia Auckett
Introduction by Eva Reich, M.D.

A fully illustrated, practical, time-tested approach to the ancient art of baby massage.

The "What's Happening to My Body?" Book for Girls
A Growing Up Guide for Parents and Daughters
Lynda Madaras, with Area Madaras
Forewords by Ralph I. Lopez, M.D., and Cynthia W. Cooke, M.D.

Selected as a "Best Book for Young Adults, 1983" by the American Library Association, this carefully researched book provides detailed explanations of what takes place in a girl's body as she grows up.

The "What's Happening to My Body?" Book for Boys
A Growing Up Guide for Parents and Sons
Lynda Madaras, with Dane Saavedra
Foreword by Ralph I. Lopez, M.D.

Written with the same candor, humor, and clarity as her puberty book for girls, Madaras' book for parents and their sons provides much-needed information on the special problems boys face during puberty.

Your Child At Play: Birth to One Year
                                One to Two Years
                                Two to Three Years
Marilyn Segal, Ph.D., and Don Adcock, Ph.D.

A three-volume series of books that enhance communication between parent and child. "Insightful, warm, and practical, these books provide expert knowledge that's a must for every parent."—T. Berry Brazelton, M.D.

(more)

Ask for these titles at your local bookstore or Order Today

Use this coupon or write to: Newmarket Press, 3 East 48th Street, New York, NY 10017. (212) 832–3575

Please send me:

____ BABY MASSAGE ($6.95, paperback)

____ THE "WHAT'S HAPPENING TO MY BODY?" BOOK FOR GIRLS ($14.95, hardcover)

____ THE "WHAT'S HAPPENING TO MY BODY?" BOOK FOR GIRLS ($ 8.95, paperback)

____ THE "WHAT'S HAPPENING TO MY BODY?" BOOK FOR BOYS ($14.95, hardcover)

____ THE "WHAT'S HAPPENING TO MY BODY?" BOOK FOR BOYS ($ 8.95, paperback)

____ YOUR CHILD AT PLAY: BIRTH TO ONE YEAR ($14.95, hardcover)

____ YOUR CHILD AT PLAY: BIRTH TO ONE YEAR ($ 8.95, paperback)

____ YOUR CHILD AT PLAY: ONE TO TWO YEARS ($14.95, hardcover)

____ YOUR CHILD AT PLAY: ONE TO TWO YEARS ($ 8.95, paperback)

____ YOUR CHILD AT PLAY: TWO TO THREE YEARS ($14.95, hardcover)

____ YOUR CHILD AT PLAY: TWO TO THREE YEARS ($ 8.95, paperback)

____ HOW DO WE TELL THE CHILDREN? ($14.95, hardcover)

Add $1.50 per order to cover shipping and handling. Allow 2–3 weeks for delivery. NY residents add applicable state and local sales tax.

I enclose a check or money order payable to Newmarket Press in the amount of $_____.

NAME _____

ADDRESS _____

CITY/STATE/ZIP _____

For quotes on quantity purchases, or for a free copy of our catalog, write or phone Newmarket Press, 3 East 48th Street, New York, NY 10017. (212) 832–3575.